Contents

Figures

BEGINNING YOUR FAMILY HISTORY

George Pelling

SIXTH EDITION

Published by
Federation of Family History Societies (Publications) Ltd
The Benson Room, Birmingham and Midland Institute,
Margaret Street, Birmingham B3 3BS, UK

Copyright © George Pelling

First published 1980
Sixth Edition 1995

ISBN 1-86006-004-8

Printed and bound at the Alden Press, Oxford

Acknowledgements

Acknowledgements for the first five editions are contained in each. The same cover has been used for all editions, except the first; my thanks to Derek Palgrave, who prepared the artwork and the script for Figure 5. I would like to thank the staff of the West Sussex Record Office, where much of my research has been done. The Inventory shown in Figure 16 is reproduced by their kind permission. The reproductions of the census returns in Figures 12 and 13 are with the permission of H.M.S.O. for which my thanks.

My thanks are also due to the following for responding so readily to requests for up to date information:-
Geoff. Mawlam and Steve Young [The Genealogical Society of Utah].
OPCS — General Registry Office, St Catherines House.
Principal Registry Office of the Family Division, Somerset House.
General Register Office for Scotland.
General Register Office for Northern Ireland.
General Register Office for Eire.
The Registrar for Jersey.
The Registrar for the Isle of Man.
Her Majesty's Greffier, Guernsey.

A special thanks to Pauline Saul [the Federation's Administrator] for assistance with research at the time of my illness and for her computer expertise.

As always, I must express my everlasting gratitude to my beloved wife for her patience and understanding in allowing me to devote so much time to Family History. Her strength and devotion at a critical time in my life has given me the inspiration to finish this work.

George Pelling

Introduction

When I talk about my absorbing interest in Family History, the question sometimes arises – "Why do you do it?"

Family History research has been described as a cross between a good detective story and a jig-saw puzzle. Certainly the thrill of the chase is experienced whilst searching and there is a great satisfaction when a particularly elusive ancestor is found and put in his allotted place on the Family Tree.

Gradually changing social conditions have given rise to a society in which many people live away from their places of origin and some find it difficult to relate to their present environment. It is a natural step for them to start searching for their "roots" and perhaps explains why family history has become so popular, particularly in America, where it is the most pursued pastime, and there is also a great interest in our other former colonies in Canada, Australia and New Zealand. There are, however, many whose families have been in the same area for generations and they obviously have a different motivation. Man has an inherent curiosity about himself and his origins and much contemporary conversation revolves around gossip about the family, neighbours and friends.

In 1982 I appeared in a Granada TV series of 5 programmes and in 1985 in a small "slot" on another programme. Following each I received hundreds of letters from all over the North West region, from people of all ages and all walks of life.

Each of us is a product of genetic and environmental influences and by studying our ancestors we can find out more about ourselves. As Don Steele has pointed out in *Discovering Your Family History* ". . . history is not merely a chronicle of past events but an enquiry into the thoughts and actions of people in the past." A closer understanding of our predecessors can be achieved by studying the history of the family, the fundamental social unit, than by the more traditional approaches to national and local history, he justifiably asserts.

Whatever the reason, the veritable explosion of interest in the subject in recent years is remarkable. When the Federation of Family History Societies was founded in 1974, it had less than a dozen members: by 1994 this total had increased to more than 170, spread across the English speaking world. I little thought, when I wrote the introduction to the First Edition in 1980, that fourteen years (and some 80,000 copies) later, I would be writing a Sixth.

The aim of the book remains unchanged, to provide the beginner with the preliminary information necessary to research back to the 16th century: by answering, for each main subject covered, the questions: When? What? Where? How? and Cost?. The order in which the subjects are considered will, it is hoped, help keep the costs to a minimum.

The number of ancestors doubles with each generation as you proceed backwards, 4 grandparents, 8 great grandparents and so on, so that 10 generations back (say 300 years) you may have as many as 1,024 ancestors; at 1066 (30 generations) the nominal number would exceed 1,000 million, but of course, thousands of names would be repeated thousands of times.

Your efforts will be rewarded by finding new relatives and if you follow the steps in this book you should be able to "do-it-yourself". The most rewarding aspect of this fascinating and absorbing pastime, for me, however, was unexpected. Since I set out to find my ancestors I have met many people, and have corresponded with many more, engaged on a similar quest. Although my search was in the past, I found fellowship and friendship in the present. May you be as fortunate.

GEORGE PELLING
January 1995

Figure 1 FAMILY QUESTIONNAIRE FORM

	Your Name	Your Husband's/Wife's Name
Please give full names	. . . .	. . . .
Previous surname(s) where appropriate		
Date/place birth	. . . .	. . . .
Date/place marriage	. . . .	. . . .
Occupation	. . . .	. . . .
Your Childrens' names*	1. . . . . 2.	3. . . . .
Date/place birth	. . . .	. . . .
Date/place marriage	. . . .	. . . .
Name of wife/husband	. . . .	. . . .
Their children*	1.	. . . .
*(if more than three	2.	. . . .
use additional sheet)	3.	. . . .

	Your Father	Your Mother (maiden name)
Date/place birth/bapt	. . . .	. . . .
Date/place marriage	. . . .	. . . .
Date/place death/bur	. . . .	. . . .
Occupation/Religion	. . . .	. . . .
Your brothers/sisters*	1. . . . . 2.	3. . . . .
Date/place birth/bapt	. . . .	. . . .
Date/place marriage	. . . .	. . . .
Name of wife/husband	. . . .	. . . .
Occupation	. . . .	. . . .
Their children*	1.	. . . .
	2.	. . . .
	3.	. . . .

	Paternal Grandparents	Maternal Grandparents
Names	. . . .	. . . .
Date/place birth/bapt	. . . .	. . . .
Date/place marriage	. . . .	. . . .
Date/place death/bur	. . . .	. . . .
Occupation/Religion	. . . .	. . . .
Any other information	. . . .

. . . .

. . . .

Your address . . . .

. . . . Telephone . . . .

1. The Starting Point — Family Sources

Many excellent Family Histories have been written which are sadly deficient in one respect: very little is known about the author, who assumed, modestly but wrongly, that no one was ever going to be interested in him. The golden rule is to start with yourself and work backwards, generation by generation, proving each step as far as possible by reference to the records available. These will be considered briefly in the following pages.

Do not take a person from the past with your name and try to trace his descendants in the hope that you may be one of them; even if there is a family legend that he is your ancestor. You may find, as you proceed, that your ancestral name several generations back is different from what it is today.

Your first sources are the memories of your immediate family and their treasures lovingly preserved over the years. Talk to all your relatives, in particular the older generation. If you can tape-record them, do so, and be prepared to jog their memories by asking questions, but mostly listen. If recording is not possible, note what they say and try to persuade them to write down their memories. They will enjoy the experience; you will find the results fascinating reading. Memory fades and needs stimulation, so you may not obtain all the information at once. Ask some more questions after a lapse of time, when they have had the opportunity for further reflection. Your relatives may live far away and you may have to rely on correspondence, but if your enquiries are vague the replies will be likewise. It is a good idea to send them a questionnaire (see Figure 1) to ensure you get all the essential information but make sure your relative knows who you are and why you need these details. Look for the following: Family Bible; letters; memorial cards; Birth, Marriage and Death Certificates; Professional Certificates; Birthday Books; Newspaper cuttings (often obituary notices are kept); Samplers (pieces of embroidery worked by young girls to demonstrate proficiency and often framed and displayed); Medals (look at the edge for name, rank and number); Photographs, about which a special word. How many times have you looked at old photos and asked who do they depict? Try to identify them and write the names lightly on the back. It is possible, although slightly expensive, to rephotograph old faded prints and produce a clear enlarged picture. Good photocopiers will produce reasonable facsimiles.

Sometimes relatives are reluctant to talk about a particular person and there may be a family "skeleton in the cupboard". Be prepared to find illegitimacy, which occurs in nearly every family.

The main source of family information for my maternal grandmother's family, and the inspiration for my starting on the quest for my ancestors was my Aunt Bess, my mother's elder, unmarried sister, who remembered her great-grandfather, born 1815, and told me the names of his 11 children and 65 grandchildren. It was some years, however, before she told me that she had destroyed her mother's marriage certificate, because the date was less than nine months before her own birth date.

It was 14 years afterwards, in 1984, that I finally located the family bible, or to be accurate that the holder contacted me, via another relative. The moral is obvious, ALL known relatives should be contacted, however remote. My research had not been wasted (research, even that which yields negative information, rarely is), because I was able to prove that one of the entries, (which covered 7 generations from 1765), was inaccurate: confusion having arisen from a marriage of cousins with the same name. So, how had the error occurred? Quite simply, the Bible was not published until 1846; prior entries had been made from memory, which emphasises that ALL sources must be checked for accuracy. Moreover, no one should be accepted as an ancestor unless and until it is proved beyond all reasonable doubt.

Try and find out where your ancestors were buried. Gravestones are an invaluable source for clarifying family relationships and often include information about several generations, which may save you the cost of purchasing birth certificates (see Chapter 5). Stones become worn and the older ones are difficult to read. Record what you can, leaving spaces where words are not clear and indicate where you have made a guess.

e.g. JOHN SMITH(ER?)S died January (?)th 18(53?), Aged 6(5?)

Look for graves in the vicinity bearing the same surname. Families often purchased adjacent plots.

Burial grounds for non-conformists were started in the 17th century and increased in number in the 18th. Public cemeteries were started in London in 1827, but most date from the 1850's or later. Most have well indexed records.

The records for a cemetery still in use will normally be found at the Office at the cemetery. The Register will normally record dates of death and burial, in addition to name, address, occupation and age of the deceased. A grave number will be given, from which the plot can be located from the grave map.

Recognising their unique value, dedicated individuals and public spirited organisations have recorded Monumental Inscriptions and the Society of Genealogists (S.O.G.) has built up a substantial collection. This invaluable work received a tremendous boost in 1978 when the Federation launched an ambitious plan to record all the inscriptions in churchyards and other burial grounds, concentrating first on those most at risk. This ideal target has not yet been fully achieved, but the response from member Societies has been magnificent. Most Societies have appointed a co-ordinator to control the recording of Monumental

Inscriptions and other projects. If you are able to help, your local Society would like to hear from you; no expertise is required. Usually the results are indexed, which saves valuable searching time, and increasingly more and more are being published, mainly by Family History Societies.

If the churchyard or burial ground in which your ancestor was buried has been landscaped, or otherwise destroyed, the inscriptions may (should, if after 1906) have been recorded, although often in a disappointingly brief manner. Your local library may have a copy.

Dates on tombstones (like dates in most records) cannot be relied upon as the stone may have been erected years after the first interment; remember also that the stone is a memorial, which means that all those listed may not be buried there.

Bibliography

Notes on the Recording of Monumental Inscriptions, J.L. Rayment, FFHS.

Family History in Focus, ed. Don Steel and Lawrence Taylor.

Relationships

Not everyone is clear about family relationships, particularly cousins. The chart shown in Figure 2 on page 12 looks daunting but it is essentially very simple, provided you follow the rules step by step. You will know that first cousins have common grandparents; if you did not it can be ascertained from the chart. The key to understanding it is to substitute yourself and your relatives in place of the symbols.

Key to Figure 2.

CA = Common Ancestor.
Relationship with Common Ancestor:- C = Child: GC = Grandchild: GGC = Great-Grandchild:
Number X = Times Great (e.g. 3 X GGC = Great-Great-Great Grandchild.).
Relationship between relatives with a common ancestor:- s = sibling (brother or sister): n = nephew/niece:
c = cousin: gn = grand-nephew/niece: number r = time removed (e.g. 1c1r = first cousin once removed).

Figure 2 RELATIONSHIP CHART

		H	1	2	3	4	5
	CA $\longrightarrow$		C	GC	GGC	2 × GGC	3 × GGC
V $\downarrow$							
1	C			s	n	gn	ggn	2 × ggn
2	GC			n	1c	1c1r	1c2r	1c3r
3	GGC			gn	1c1r	2c	2c1r	2c2r
4	2 × GGC			ggn	1c2r	2c1r	3c	3c1r
5	3 × GGC			2 × ggn	1c3r	2c2r	3c1r	4c

E.g. The following abridged Family Tree shows Alfred and Annie, who are the Common ancestors of their daughters, Margaret and Nora; their grandchildren, George and Alice and their Great-grandchildren, Nichola and Janet.

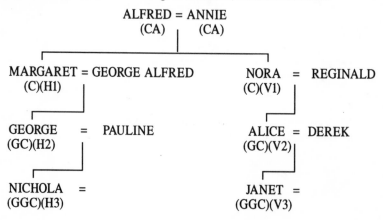

The application of the chart to the persons on the tree will demonstrate how it works.

E.g. 1. George and Alice have common grandparents; Therefore, place George at H2 = GC. Place Alice at V2 = GC. Their relationship is stated where columns H2 and V2 intersect, i.e. 1C [first cousin].

E.g. 2. What is the relationship of George to Alice's daughter, Janet? Not second cousin, as is commonly supposed. George is H2 [GC], as before; is V3[GGC]: H2 and V3 intersect at 1c1r {first cousin once removed]. Logical enough, since Janet is one generation removed from George's first cousin Alice. It is of course Nichola and Janet who are second cousins.

(NB: The chart can be extended indefinitely: cousins will always be on the diagonal from top left to bottom right.) Prince Charles and Princess Diana have a common ancestor, James I of England. He is 11 X. GGC and she 10 X. GGC: what is their relationship? Extending the chart, he would be in column H13 and she in column V12; they are therefore 11th cousins once removed: if you don't believe me, extend the chart and check it!.

2. Setting Your Sights

Being Selective

Start immediately to fill in a Pedigree Chart (sometimes called a Birth Brief) as far back as you can. A sample chart is shown in Figure 3, which provides spaces for all your ancestors back to your 16 Great-great-grandparents. The most important thing is to decide next is which of the possible options you should choose, otherwise you will simply be ancestor collecting with no objective in view. Your choice will be influenced by the data you have immediately available. You may, of course, change your mind later, when you have obtained more material and as you become more familiar with the subject, but you should be aware of the following possibilities at an early stage, since this may influence your approach.

One Name

The researcher collects every reference to a particular surname, wherever and whenever it occurs.

Total Ancestry

Having traced 16 great-great-grandparents, the researcher then looks for their 32 parents, so that every time an ancestor is found he starts looking for two more.

Several Families

The objective is to research a number of families (perhaps those of your 4 grand-parents) in depth, by putting them into their local and historical context, with perhaps, the ultimate aim of writing a family history.

Seeking Help

The previously stated aim of this book is to show you how to do it yourself, but, however independent and dedicated you may be, you will need help.

Visit your local library, with which you may already be familiar (though perhaps not with the Reference section of it), where you will find copies of at least some of the material mentioned in the following pages. A list of helpful books appears at the end of this and subsequent chapters. Library books are arranged under code numbers: those listed and most others useful to a Family Historian will be found under code 929. The library notice board should have details of local societies and particulars of any further education classes covering the subject.

Mention has already been made of the Federation of Family History Societies and a current list of member societies is included on the back cover of its magazine Family History News and Digest, which is published twice a year.

There is almost certainly a society covering the area in which you live and membership subscriptions are modest (usually £5-£10 per annum). You do not have to be an expert to join; everyone is welcome, especially beginners. Your ancestors may be from a different part of the country and you may feel that your local society is remote from your areas of interest, but most societies produce a quarterly journal, which they exchange with other societies, thus building up a library of material from outside their immediate region. Additionally, most societies hold monthly meetings (except for, perhaps, a summer break) and have speakers on a variety of subjects, national as well as local. Most importantly, you will meet fellow family historians who have experienced the same problems and may be able to help you overcome them. I write from personal experience: in 1973 my employer decided that my services were required in Lancashire. I have no known ancestors north of Felixstowe, but joined the local Society, of which I successively became Treasurer, Projects Co-Ordinator, Chairman and Vice-President.

The Federation has an Administrator, c/o the Benson Room,Birmingham and Midland Institute, Margaret Street, Birmingham, B3 3BS, who will gladly provide a list, upon request. The address of the society secretary may not be close to where you live but do not let that deter you from seeking further information; most societies have more than one meeting venue, some of the larger ones have as many as 11 branches: for example the old county of Lancashire is covered by 4 societies, which between them have no fewer than 20 meeting places.

There are an ever growing number of One Name Societies and individuals who specialise in particular names. To find out whether yours is amongst the thousands now covered, apply to The Registrar, Guild of One Name Studies, Box G, 14 Charterhouse Buildings, Goswell Road, London EC1M 7BA for a copy of their prospectus.

This is an appropriate point to mention that when writing to anyone, from whom a reply is required, always enclose a stamped, addressed envelope, (of at least A5 size), or if writing from overseas send 3 International Reply Coupons, which are obtainable at the Post Office.

Figure 3 **BIRTH BRIEF**

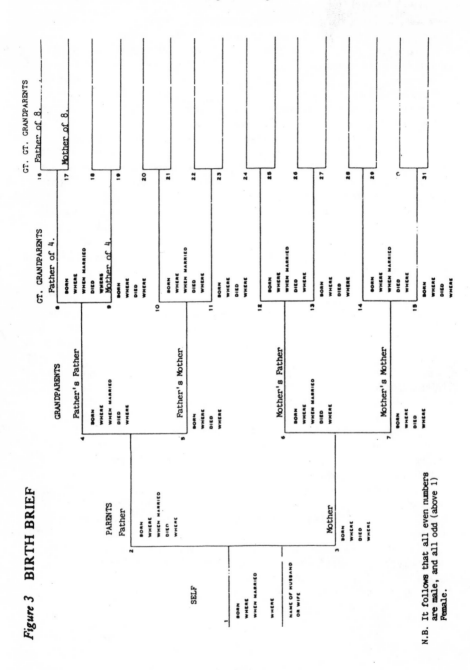

N.B. It follows that all even numbers are male, and all odd (above 1) Female.

16

Figure 4 FAMILY GROUP SHEET

Chart Number _____

Name _____ Source

Born _____ at _____ _____

Baptised _____ at _____ _____

Married _____ at _____ _____

Died _____ at _____ _____

Buried _____ at _____ _____

Occupation _____ _____

Chart Number _____

Father's name _____ Source

Born _____ at _____ _____

Baptised _____ at _____ _____

Married _____ at _____ _____

Died _____ at _____ _____

Buried _____ at _____ _____

Buried _____ at _____ _____

Occupation _____ _____

Chart Number _____

Mother (maiden name) _____ Source

Born _____ at _____ _____

Baptised _____ at _____ _____

Died _____ at _____ _____

Buried _____ at _____ _____

Occupation _____ _____

Children in order of birth

                                            Source   Chart No.

1. _____ born _____ at _____ _____ _____
2. _____ born _____ at _____ _____ _____
3. _____ born _____ at _____ _____ _____
4. _____ born _____ at _____ _____ _____
5. _____ born _____ at _____ _____ _____
6. _____ born _____ at _____ _____ _____
7. _____ born _____ at _____ _____ _____
8. _____ born _____ at _____ _____ _____
9. _____ born _____ at _____ _____ _____
10. _____ born _____ at _____ _____ _____

3. Handling Data

It is obvious that the Pedigree Chart, already considered, only has sufficient space to record the essential basic data:

Birth/baptism, Marriage, death/burial, with the dates of each. Other information can be included on Family Group Sheets, as illustrated in Figure 4.

You will, however, collect a lot of other material and secondary records will be necessary. No two family historians will ever agree about the best methods of recording additional information, but some generally agreed principles can be stated.

(a) Start recording your information immediately.
(b) Be methodical and be honest. Acknowledge family indiscretions.
(c) Always identify your source and date you made your search.
(d) A research record is as essential as a statement of the results.

List source searched, dates covered and the names for which you have looked, plus place and date of search:

e.g. Parish Register, Rudgwick (Sx), Bapts. Ms 1760-1812: Burs. 1781-1812. All PELLING entries: BRIDGER, pre 1802. 3/12/80 W.SX.R.O. (Microfilm).

This note illustrates some other recommended practices:

(i) Use capital letters for SURNAMES, particularly vital for families where surnames are also used as christian names.
(ii) (Sx) = Sussex, Place names should indicate the county, in case of duplication elsewhere. For example, you know that the Preston you researched was in Lancashire but it might not be obvious to anyone following, who might have to consider the 10 in other counties.
(iii) Conventional abbreviations (see pages 19–20) have been used in noting the records. This practice should not, however, be extended to the names: the converse also applies, e.g. Jo. found in an archive, should be recorded as such, not as John or Joseph, because that is what you assume it to be.
(e) It is just as important to record negative results. e.g. M.I.s (i.e.Monumental Inscriptions) St. James. Haslingden (Lancs) 23/9/1979; No MUSKIEs.
(f) Whatever system you adopt must be flexible so that additional information can be added, as found. A loose leaf system is therefore recommended and a ring binder larger than A4 will probably be required to accommodate the larger documents you may expect to accumulate.

Opinion is divided regarding the use of index cards; it depends upon what you want the index for and whether it is the best way for you to achieve your retrieval objective. However, the advent of computers has liberated many family historians from the constraints of card or other paper indexing. Your choice of computer will be governed by your pocket and if you purchased one for your children, without knowing much about it about it, you are stuck with what you have. If, however, you do not already have one, there is one golden rule to observe before making your choice. First consider the software available and whether it will produce what you require. At University I have recently had to come to terms with the computer, but at my mature age I found it difficult. The best advice I can give is that advice should be sought from an experienced person.

(g) Records must be cross referenced. Families should be kept separate, either in distinct sections of the folder, or in separate folders. The same people will occur in both sections and you need to be able to refer easily from one to the other. The following symbols and conventions are those most widely used:

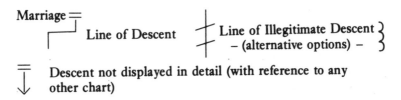

Marriage —

⌐ Line of Descent

┼ Line of Illegitimate Descent ⎫
– (alternative options) – ⎬

⇊ Descent not displayed in detail (with reference to any other chart)

Abbreviations

about, approximately	circa or c.
bachelor	bach.
baptised	bapt.
Bishops Transcripts	BTs
born	b.
buried	bur.
century	cent. (e.g. 18th cent. or C 18)
Codicil	Cod.
Co-heir	Co-h.
Court	Ct.
dated	dat.
daughter	dau.
died	d. or obit.
died childless	d.s.p. or o.s.p.
died unmarried	d. unm.
divorced	div.
educated at	educ.
eldest	eld.

father	f.
grandfather	g.f.
great-grandfather	g-g.f.
heir	h.
infant	inf.
inventory	inv.
junior	jnr.
Letters of Administration	Admon.
licence	lic.
living	liv. (e.g. liv. 1634)
married	m. (or sometimes marr.)
Monumental Inscription	M.I.
of this parish	o.t.p.
Parish Register	P.R.
Prerogative Court of Canterbury	P.C.C.
Prerogative Court of York	P.C.Y.
Public Record Office	P.R.O.
son	s.
time of	temp (e.g. temp Henry V)
widow	wid.
widower	wdr.
wife	w.
Will proved	Will pr.

Charts and Group Sheets are fine for recording data but not for visual display. Eventually, you will probably wish to put your information into Family Tree form, although many competent family historians shirk from doing so because of the severe problems of draughtsmanship involved.

The most used (in many cases misused, would be a more accurate description) method is the line pedigree. Most of the pitfalls of confusion and inadequacy of data can be avoided if, once again, certain basic rules are followed.

1. Names of the same generation should be kept at the same level.
2. Lines of descent should be drawn from the marriage symbol; (as shown in Figure 5).
3. Brief narrative informative may be added below the name, but the whole purpose and effect of the line pedigree is nullified if it is cluttered with too much detail, which is better recorded elsewhere.
4. Where there is more than one marriage, clearly indicate that fact next to the marriage symbol.
   E.gs: = (1), indicates one or more further marriages.
        = (2), indicates second marriage.
5. Normally record children in strict order of birth, from left to right. However, it may be necessary to depart from this rule, (if so indicate by numbering the

children) e.g. where cousins marry, in order not to break the next rule, which should be regarded as inviolate.

6. Never, ever, create confusion by crossing pedigree lines.
7. Record only information which has been verified, which does not mean copying from printed sources, without checking, as far as possible, the original sources. If simply copied, then that should be stated. E.g. (per "title of publication" and its date).

Bibliography

How to Record Your Family Tree, Patrick Palgrave-Moore.

Computers for Family History — An Introduction, David Hawgood.

Figure 5 LINE PEDIGREE

John Pelling = (1) Lydia

bapt. 4 Nov 1735 Itchingfield (Sx)
bur. 15 Feb. 1803 Rudgwick (Sx)

b. 1738/39
bur. 9 May 1790 Rudgwick (Sx)

Jose Pelling = Hannah Bridger

bapt. 22 Jan 1769 Iichingfield (Sx)
bur 21 Jun 1835 Rudgwick (Sx)

bapt. 17 May 1782 Rudgwick
m. 20 Apr 1802 Rudgwick
d. Petworth Workhouse (Sx)
bur. 22 Feb 1860 Rudgwick

Michael Pelling = Ann Burfoot

bapt. 6 Jun 1818 Rudgwick
d. 17 Apr 1861 Ewhurst (Sy)

bapt. 13 Jan 1819 Horsham (Sx)
m. 17 Mar 1846 Horsham

Alexander Pelling = Sarah Jane Penfold

b. 10 Jul 1855 Ewhurst
d. 23 Nov 1936 Ockley (Sy)

b. 28 Jan 1863 Ifield (Sx)
m. 13 Jan 1895 Dorking (Sy)
d. 2 Dec 1951 Ockley (Sy)

George Alfred Pelling = Margaret R. Passiful

b. 11 Apr 1895 Dorking
d. 22 Mar 1970 Brighton (Sx)

b. 26 Jul 1904 Portslade (Sx)
m. 1 Oct 1932 Portslade
d. 14 Oct 1984 Chichester (Sx)

George Pelling = Pauline Winifrid Holden

b. 25 Jun 1933 Ockley

b. 30 May 1938 Upminster (Essex)
m. 19 Aug 1961 West Blatchington (Sx)

Nichola

b. 16 Oct 1963
Walthamstow
London

Roger

b. 25 Feb 1965
d. 25 Feb 1965
Orpington (Kt)

Malcolm

b. 28 Oct 1966
Farnborough (Kt)

David

b. 1 Jun 1970
Farnborough (Kt)

4. Who Has Been Here Before Me?

There is only space here to indicate briefly some of the sources available which may be consulted to find out not only what has been done before but also what is being done now.

Genealogists have sometimes spent years researching a family only to discover that a substantial pedigree already exists. If you find one, however, your task is not over, it has simply been made easier. All printed and manuscript pedigrees should be checked against the original records for authenticity and accuracy and also checked for completeness. Many printed pedigrees were compiled in the nineteenth century when, it is probably true to say, standards of proof were lower than we would consider acceptable today. Some of the pedigrees were prepared for people of standing and "inconvenient" ancestors may have been deliberately omitted. if, however, you approach such pedigrees with the necessary scepticism, invaluable information can be obtained.

Indexes of printed pedigrees are contained in the following books:

The Genealogist's Guide	G.W. Marshall (prior to 1903)
A Genealogical Guide	J.B. Whitmore (1900-1950)
The Genealogist's Guide	G.B. Barrow (1950-1977)

The dates in brackets indicate the dates between which the pedigrees were printed not the dates the pedigrees cover (e.g. a pedigree from the 16th century to 1890 printed in 1956 would be indexed in Barrow and not in Marshall.)

Burke's Peerage and *Burke's Landed Gentry* contain many printed pedigrees. If you have an ancestor who achieved some distinction in his own field, then he may be listed in *Who Was Who?*, which contains biographical information. More detailed information may also be available in *The Dictionary of National Biography.*

The Society of Genealogists, 14 Charterhouse Buildings, Goswell Road, London EC1M 7BA, has a large collection of manuscript pedigrees in its substantial library and there are also many deposited in local libraries and county record offices.

The largest collection of pedigrees is held, however, in the form of Family Group Sheets (approximately 8,000,000, by The Church of Jesus Christ of Latter-Day Saints (Mormons), at their main family history library at Salt Lake City, Utah, U.S.A. In addition their International Genealogical Index (IGI) compiled by computer has revolutionised genealogical research in recent years. Books published before the IGI became available suggest that civil registration (see next Chapter) is the first record to research. Since, however, registration certificates have to be purchased it is prudent to consult the IGI first if you are seeking a baptism or marriage before 1875, which is the latest year covered. It should be mentioned that the number of baptisms is much greater than the marriage entries (indexed under both names) and burials are not included except for a minimal number of infants. Marriages known to be included in a printed index elsewhere are not included.

The number of entries which cover not only England, Scotland, Ireland, Wales, Isle of Man and Channel Islands but also many European countries and America, is staggering; the most recent version, (at the time of writing) containins over 187,000,000 names. The index is on microfiche, small sheets of microfilm about 4 by 6 inches, each containing 16,000 to 17,000 names. The fiche is inserted into a reader, which is very simple to operate. U.K. names are arranged by county, alphabetically by surname, then by given name, and then chronologically, the earliest date being 1538. The latest technological development is the transfer of the index onto compact disc, that is part of 'Family Search' [the computerised system in the Family History Library in Salt Lake City; it is also available at the Church's Family History Centres in the UK]. With this index countrywide (instead of county) searches are possible.

The Latter-Day Saint's Family History libraries in the United Kingdom, [see Appendix I] have the full index. You do not have to be a member of their church to use their libraries, which are freely open to all; no visitor need fear that any attempt to convert them will be made. Libraries are staffed by volunteers and have restricted opening hours, which should be ascertained when planning a visit.

The Society of Genealogists also has the full index, as do an increasing number of the larger family history societies. Many County Record Offices have the index for their county, which may also be found in the main reference libraries. It must be emphasised that the IGI is an index and, like any other index contains errors. It has been prepared not only from printed sources but also from entries submitted by members of the church and they, like all of us, must be expected to have made some mistakes. All indexes are the tools of genealogical research and not a substitute for it; once an entry is found in any index it should be checked by reference to the original record.

The Latter-Day Saints also maintain The Family Registry, another microfiche index, containing names being researched and by whom.

Most Family History Societies have published Registers of their Members' Interests, which show the names being researched, together with their location and dates, and the name and address of the researcher. Some societies have banded together to produce a larger, Regional Directory, e.g. the North West Societies usually update their Members' interests between publications of their Register, by printing the names being researched by new members in their journal.

There are also national and international directories, produced annually.

Mention has been made of the Society of Genealogists' Library, which is open to non-members on payment of a fee. The scale, at the time of writing is:

1 hour	£3.00
Half day	£7.50
Day	£10.00

Obviously, if you contemplate using the library on a regular basis, it will be cheaper to join the Society, for which the current subscription rates are:

Entrance fee on first joining	£7.50
Annual: Town members (residing within	
25 miles from Trafalgar Square)	£30.00
Others (U.K.) & overseas)	£21.00

Reduced rates are available for married couples and students under 25 years of age.

Courses for beginners are run twice yearly, in the spring and the autumn.

The library houses a general slip index of some 3,000,000 names, an index of Chancery and other Court proceedings, with about 4,500,000 references prior to 1800, and has a microfilm collection of nearly 2,500 reels. It also has an extensive collection of printed and typed family histories.

Other contents of this superb library will be described in later Chapters dealing with the subject matter covered.

Opening times: Tuesdays, Fridays and Saturdays: 10 a.m. – 6 p.m.
Wednesdays and Thursdays: 10 a.m. – 8 p.m.

It is closed on Mondays, Bank Holidays and the Friday afternoons and Saturdays preceding. It is also closed for stocktaking in the week of the first Monday in February.

Bibliography

Burke's Family Index, which is an index of names in:

Burke's Landed Gentry and Burke's Peerage and Baronetage.

Who Was Who?

Dictionary of National Biography

Unpublished Personal Name Indexes in Record Offices and Libraries, J.S.W. Gibson, FFHS.

5. Civil Registration

England and Wales

All births, marriages and deaths since 1 July 1837 are supposed to have been registered by the State, but in the earlier years some escaped the net. The country is divided into Registration Districts under the control of a Superintendent Registrar, and Districts are divided into Sub-Districts. Certificates are available from the Registrar only at the time of registration or shortly afterwards; once a register is filled it is sent to the Superintendent Registrar from whom certificates have to be obtained. Usually the indexes of the records (but not the records themselves), which, of course, relate only to events which occurred within that district, may be examined.

(i) Births and deaths are reported to the Registrar by individuals, usually close relatives.

(ii) Marriages:

Church of England. The officiating clergyman is responsible for notifying the Registrar immediately. Since 1837 two copies of the Anglican marriage registers have been kept by the incumbents. When full, one is retained by the Church and the other deposited with the registrar. The register for a small parish in which there are few marriages per year may take years to complete and the Superintendent may, therefore, not have a copy of the register. The record keeping methods in local offices make it difficult to trace a marriage unless the church is known.

Other Denominations. The Registrar either attends the ceremony or is notified. Civil Marriages are registered when they are performed.

If you are sure that your ancestors came from a particular area within a given Registration District then it may be easier, quicker and more convenient to search locally. First obtain an application form and fill it in as far as possible. If you do not know the exact date you are entitled to ask the Registrar to search for a 5-year period. If, for example, you are looking for a birth you think occurred in 1858 you might choose to ask for the years 1856–1860 to be searched; if you are certain that it was not before 1858 then you could request a search for the years 1858 to 1862 inclusive. A full (not short) certificate should always be requested; the present cost is £5.50.

Register Offices do not have sufficient staff to undertake indefinite or protracted searches. If such a search is required then a general search in the indexes may be made personally, but it is costly, £13 for any number of successive hours not exceeding six. If you are uncertain whether the entry you have found is the correct one you may ask the staff to verify it by reference to the records. The general search fee covers the cost of 8 verifications: a charge of £2.50 is payable for each subsequent reference checked, unless a certificate is issued from the entry checked, in which case only the certificate fee is charged.

Before undertaking a general search locally, however, you should consider the advantages of making a general search of the National Indexes of births marriages and deaths. Until comparatively recently, there was little choice but to travel to London to consult the indexes, or to get someone to do it for you. Microfilm copies are now available at many libraries and record offices, but most of the local indexes are incomplete. Those held by the Family History Centres of the Church of Jesus Christ of Latter-day Saints (see Appendix I) have complete indexes.

The full national indexes are housed at St. Catherine's House, Kingsway, London, WC8 6JP, (phone 0171-242-0262), which can be inspected free of charge and no reader's ticket is required. Opening hours are Monday—Friday 8.30 a.m.—4.30 p.m.

Separate Indexes are kept for Births, Marriages and Deaths. There are four quarterly indexes for each year ending: 31 March, 30 June, 30 September and 31 December. It is important to note that the date in the index is the date of registration NOT the date when the event took place. It may, therefore, be necessary to search the following quarter even when the precise date is known. Thus a birth on December 26 may not have been registered until the first quarter of the following year. The index shows the Registration district, volume and page number. There may be two or more entries for the same name and you may not know in which county the place of registration is located. This can be ascertained from the list in Figure 6. E.g. 8a for the year 1860 is Cheshire. If you are uncertain whether the reference you have found in the index relates to the person you are seeking then the staff will verify it for you within a few days by reference to the records on payment of £3.00. Once you have found the entry which you believe is the one you want, a simple form must be completed. Unless you can return for the certificate on the fourth subsequent working day you will be asked to self-address an envelope so that it can be posted to you. A priority service is available upon payment of an additional fee of £14.50 whereby certificates can be collected the day after application. The cost is the same as locally, £6.00. If you cannot visit St.Catherine's House to make a personal search, certificates may be applied for by post, but only a five year search can be requested and the cost is £15, of which £5.50 is refunded if the search is unsuccessful. It may therefore be cheaper to pay someone to carry out the personal search for you, if their fee is less than the difference. If, however, you obtain the precise reference, (which consists of Quarter; Year; District; Volume number; Page number), from a microfilm of the indexes, the cost is reduced to £12. Postal applications should not be sent to St. Catherine's House but to: General Register Office, Smedley Hydro, Trafalgar Rd, Southport, Merseyside, PR8 2HH.

Figure 6 CODES EMPLOYED AT ST. CATHERINE'S HOUSE

ROMAN NUMERALS 1837–1851		ARABIC WITH SMALL LETTER 1852-Aug. 1946	
I	London & Middlesex	1a	London & Middlesex
II	London & Middlesex	1b	London & Middlesex
III	London & Middlesex	1c	London & Middlesex
IV	London & Surrey	1d	London, Kent & Surrey
V	Kent	2a	Kent & Surrey
VI	Beds., Berks., Bucks., & Herts.	2b	Hants. & Sussex
VII	Hants. & Sussex	2c	Berks. & Hants.
VIII	Dorset, Hants., & Wilts	3a	Berks., Bucks., Herts., Middx. & Oxon.
IX	Cornwall & Devon	3b	Beds., Cambs., Hunts., Northants., & Suffolk
X	Devon & Somerset		
XI	Glos., Soms., & Warwicks.	4a	Essex & Suffolk
XII	Essex & Suffolk	4b	Norfolk
XIII	Norfolk & Suffolk	5a	Dorset & Wiltshire
XIV	Cambs., Hunts., & Lincs.	5b	Devonshire
XV	Leics., Northants., Notts. & Rutland.	5c	Cornwall & Somerset.
XVI	Oxon., Staffs. & Warwicks.	6a	Glos., Herefords. & Salop
XVII	Staffordshire	6b	Staffs., Warwicks. & Worcs.
XVIII	Glos., Salop., Staffs., Warwicks., & Worcs.	6c	Warwicks., & Worcestershire
XIX	Cheshire, Derbys. & Flints.	6d	Warwickshire
XX	Lancashire	7a	Leics., Lincs. & Rutland
XXI	Lancashire & Yorkshire	7b	Derbyshire & Notts.
XXII	Yorkshire	8a	Cheshire
XXIII	Yorkshire	8b	Lancashire
XXIV	Durham & Yorkshire	8c	Lancashire
XXV	Cumberland, Lancashire, Northumberland & Westmorland	8d	Lancashire
		8e	Lancashire
XXVI	Brecknocks., Carmarthens., Glams., Herefords., Mons., Pembs., Randors. & Salop.	9a	Yorkshire
		9b	Yorkshire
		9c	Yorkshire
XXVII	Anglesey, Caernarvons., Cardigans., Denbighs., Flints., Merioneths., & Montgomeryshire	9d	Yorkshire
		10a	Durham
		10b	Cumberland, Northumberland & Westmorland
		11a	Glamorgan, Monmouth. & Pembrokeshire.
		11b	Anglesey, Brecknocks., Denbighs., Flints., Montgomeryshire & Radnorshire.

(N.B. As the older volumes (above) are
   replaced, the Roman numerals are
   being replaced by Arabic.)

Cheques and postal orders should be made payable to "The Registrar General": remittances from overseas should be by sterling money order: cash should not be sent.

Figure 7 DATA GIVEN IN BIRTH CERTIFICATES

No.	When and where born	Name if any	Sex	Name and surname of father	Name, surname and maiden name of mother	Occupation of father	Signature, description and residence of Informant	When registered	Signature of Registrar	Name entered after Registration

(N.B. Mother's maiden name not shown in indexes prior to September 1911.

It should be noted that a direct ancestor's certificate may not always be the best one to obtain. To explain this statement it is necessary to anticipate slightly the contents of the next Chapter. Census returns may be consulted (free of charge) for the years 1841, 1851, 1861, 1871, 1881 and 1891, but it is necessary to know an address. Suppose that your grandfather, Malcolm, had been born in 1866, his sister Nichola in 1863 and his brother David in 1870. The essential information you require (names of parents and mother's maiden name) will be the same on the birth certificates for all three, but by obtaining David's (instead of Malcolm's) you will have an address to check in the 1871 census. The Family is less likely to have moved in the intervening year after 1870 than in the 5 years after 1866 (or in the 5 year period 1861–1866).

Figure 8 DATA GIVEN IN MARRIAGE CERTIFICATES

No.	When married	Names & surnames of each party	Ages	Condition (e.g. Bachelor or Spinster)	Rank or Profession of each party	Residence at time of marriage	Both fathers' names & surnames	Rank or profession of both fathers
Place of marriage and ceremony performed								
Signatures of parties who were married				Signatures of witnesses				

It is easier to find a marriage, and to be certain that you are right, than to find a birth because the names of both spouses are indexed. Look for the less common name first then check it with the name of the spouse and, if the references are identical, then you have a match. (N.B. After 1912 the other spouse's name is stated in brackets.)

Figure 9 DATA GIVEN IN DEATH CERTIFICATES

No.	When & where died	Name & surname	Sex	Age (Often only approximate)	Occupation	Cause	Signature description & residence of Informant	When registered	Signature of Registrar

Figure 10 FACSIMILES OF CERTIFICATES ISSUED BY GENERAL REGISTER OFFICE

CERTIFIED COPY OF AN ENTRY OF BIRTH

The fee for this certificate is 40p. When application is made by post a handling fee is payable in addition.

GIVEN AT THE GENERAL REGISTER OFFICE, SOMERSET HOUSE, LONDON

Application Number 3716

REGISTRATION DISTRICT Hambledon

1855. BIRTH in the Sub-district of Cranley in the County of Surrey

Columns:— No.	1 When and where born	2 Name, if any	3 Sex	4 Name and surname of father	5 Name, surname and maiden surname of mother	6 Occupation of father	7 Signature, description and residence of informant	8 When registered	9 Signature of registrar	10* Name entered after registration
291	Tenth July 1855 Pitland Street Ewhurst	Alexander	Boy	Michael Pelling	Ann Pelling formerly Burfoot	Farm Labourer	X The Mark of Ann Pelling Mother Pitland Street Ewhurst	Twentieth August 1855	James Smith Registrar	—

CERTIFIED to be a true copy of an entry in the certified copy of a Register of Births in the District above mentioned.
Given at the GENERAL REGISTER OFFICE, SOMERSET HOUSE, LONDON, under the Seal of the said Office, the 30th day of June 1972

This certificate is issued in pursuance of the Births and Deaths Registration Act 1953. Section 34 provides that any certified copy of an entry purporting to be sealed or stamped with the seal of the General Register Office shall be received as evidence of the birth or death to which it relates without any further or other proof of the entry, and no certified copy purporting to have been given in the said Office shall be of any force or effect unless it is sealed or stamped as aforesaid. *See note overleaf

BX 886348

CAUTION:—Any person who (1) falsifies any of the particulars on this certificate, or (2) uses a falsified certificate as true, knowing it to be false, is liable to prosecution.

Form A502M (S.311761) Dd 833790 W.060 12/71 Hw. RE-30

GENERAL REGISTER OFFICE ENGLAND

CERTIFIED COPY OF AN ENTRY OF MARRIAGE

The fee for this certificate is 40p. When application is made by post, a handling fee is payable in addition.

Given at the GENERAL REGISTER OFFICE, SOMERSET HOUSE, LONDON

Application Number 4675 D

Registration District Horsham

1846. Marriage solemnized at the Church in the Parish of Horsham in the County of Sussex

No.	1 When married	2 Name and surname	3 Age	4 Condition	5 Rank or profession	6 Residence at the time of marriage	7 Father's name and surname	8 Rank or profession of father
251	March 17	Michael Pelling	full	Bachelor	Labourer	Horsham	John Pelling	Farmer
		Ann Burfoot	full	Spinster	—	Horsham	Alexander Burfoot	Farmer

Married in the Parish Church according to the Rites and Ceremonies of the Church of England by Banns by me

This marriage was solemnized between us, Michael Pelling, Ann Burfoot

in the presence of us, R. Collins, Elizabeth Burfoot

John E. Hodgson, Vicar

CERTIFIED to be a true copy of an entry in the certified copy of a Register of Marriages in the District above mentioned.
Given at the GENERAL REGISTER OFFICE, SOMERSET HOUSE, LONDON, under the Seal of the said Office, the 15th day of July 1972.

This certificate is issued in pursuance of section 65 of the Marriage Act 1949. Sub-section (3) of that section provides that any certified copy of an entry purporting to be sealed or stamped with the seal of the General Register Office shall be received as evidence of the marriage to which it relates without any further or other proof of the entry, and no certified copy purporting to have been given in the said Office shall be of any force or effect unless it is sealed or stamped as aforesaid.

MA 983416

CAUTION:—Any person who (1) falsifies any of the particulars on this certificate, or (2) uses a falsified certificate as true knowing it to be false, is liable to prosecution.

Form A513 (S.138669) Dd.833296 20,000 10/71 Hw.

GENERAL REGISTER OFFICE ENGLAND

CERTIFIED COPY OF AN ENTRY OF DEATH

GIVEN AT THE GENERAL REGISTER OFFICE, SOMERSET HOUSE, LONDON

Application Number 5158 D.

REGISTRATION DISTRICT Hambledon

1861. DEATH in the Sub-district of Cranley in the County of Surrey

Columns:— No.	1 When and where died	2 Name and surname	3 Sex	4 Age	5 Occupation	6 Cause of death	7 Signature, description and residence of informant	8 When registered	9 Signature of registrar
190	Seventeenth April 1861 Pitland Street Ewhurst	Michael Pelling	Male	43 Years	Farm Labourer	Pneumonia of the right Lung Certified	Ebenezer Horden In Attendance Cranley Street Cranley	Eighteenth April 1861	Edward Davey Registrar

CERTIFIED to be a true copy of an entry in the certified copy of a Register of Deaths in the District above mentioned.
Given at the GENERAL REGISTER OFFICE, SOMERSET HOUSE, LONDON, under the Seal of the said Office, the 13th day of Sept 19 73

This certificate is issued in pursuance of the Births and Deaths Registration Act 1953. Section 34 provides that any certified copy of an entry purporting to be sealed or stamped with the seal of the General Register Office shall be received as evidence of the birth or death to which it relates without any further or other proof of the entry, and no certified copy purporting to have been given in the said Office shall be of any force or effect unless it is sealed or stamped as aforesaid.

DX 190002

CAUTION:—Any person who (1) falsifies any of the particulars on this certificate, or (2) uses a falsified certificate as true, knowing it to be false, is liable to prosecution.

Form A504M (S.338344) Dd.801453 21m 12/72 Mw.

GENERAL REGISTER OFFICE ENGLAND

13/9/73

English death certificates are not very helpful genealogically except perhaps to provide an address for checking in the census returns and to give age at death from which one can compute a birth date. Often the informant is a close relative. N.B. Death Indexes from 1866 onwards give age at death, anyway.

If you do not find the entry that you expect to find at a particular date there are 3 possible reasons.

(a) The date you have is wrong — not uncommon.

Remedy — Widen your search progressively either side of the date. e.g. Believed date 1856: search 1857 and 1855, followed by 1858 and 1854 and so on.

(b) The name is different.

Remedy — Look for all possible spelling variants. Remember that your ancestor may have been illiterate and the verbal information he gave may have been misheard or misspelt. This happens with common names as well as those more unusual. A researcher in Lancashire has recorded no less than 17 different spellings of Whittaker. The difference may be much greater than a missing or extra letter. One of my grandparent's names was Passiful, which in many records appears as Percival.

(c) It was not registered.

Remedy — Try alternative records.

The birth and marriages certificates shown in Figure 10 illustrate the point made about names. The birth of ALEXANDER PELLING was registered by his mother, who, it will be seen, made her mark.

The Registrar recorded her maiden name as BIRFETT. The marriage indexes were searched backwards from 1855 for 10 years and forward for 5 (marriages do not always precede births). No marriage between MICHAEL PELLING and ANN BIRFETT was registered. Fortunately, there was only one MICHAEL PELLING who married in the period. The certificate illustrated was obtained and his wife's name proved to be BURFOOT.

The searcher did not know at the time that his Aunt, who never knew her grandparents, had a sampler completed by ANN BURFOOT in 1826. This demonstrates the importance of family information which has already been stressed. It also shows that girls who embroidered samplers including their names were not necessarily literate but may simply have copied or filled in a pattern provided.

The death certificate was important because it provided an address to look for in the 1861 census (see next chapter) without which Michael's birthplace would have more difficult to find.

Other Indexes Available at St. Catherine's House

(a) Births & Deaths at Sea, 1 July 1837–31 December 1874 (N.B. After 1874 at Registrar General for Shipping & Seamen, Llandaff, Cardiff, Wales).

(b) Births, marriages and deaths of British Citizens overseas, Consular Returns. From 1 July 1849.

(c) Army returns of Births, marriages and deaths. From 1761.
(d) R.A.F. returns of Births, marriages and deaths. From 1920.

Research in England, (unlike Scotland - see below), has been hampered by access being only to the indexes; the registers themselves being unavailable.

The system described above may be dramatically changed during the course of the next few years. In January 1990 the Government published a White Paper entitled Registration:Proposals for Change, setting out its recommendations for reform. Understandably, the Government has become increasingly concerned about the misuse of certificates obtained for various fraudulent purposes. It recommends that records over 75 years old be made available for public inspection in a record library. As it is to be privatised, a charge would be made for access to these. For records less than 75 years old, provision will be made for the issue of non-certified copies of any entries identified from the indexes. However, anyone requiring a certified copy will be required to identify themselves, give an address (which may be checked), state their relationship to the subject of the certificate and the purpose for which it is required.

It will still be possible to purchase certified copies of entries in the indexes over 75 years old, or alternatively non-certified copies. [N.B. The above paragraph was written four years ago, since when nothing has happened].

Channel Islands

Jersey

No personal Searches may be made.
Registration began August 1842.
Superintendent Registrar, States Office, 10 Royal Square, St. Helier, Jersey.
Certificates cost £5 each plus postage, £0.50 U.K., £1 elsewhere. Plus 5 year research charge — Births and deaths £5, marriages £10. Fees should be paid by sterling cheque or by British Postal Order payable to "The Treasurer of the States".

Guernsey and other Islands

Personal searches may be made at office of Registrar General, Greffe, Royal Court House, St. Peter Port, Guernsey. The registers themselves may be consulted; not just the indexes.
Registration of births and deaths commenced 1840. (Sark and Alderney 1925).
Anglican marriages 1919.
Certificates cost £3.

Isle of Man

Although registration of births was not compulsory until 1878, an Act of 1849 provided that ... 'persons who object to and decline the offices of the Established Church' . . . could register births and marriages. The earliest contemporary records therefore date from 1849 but it was also provided that earlier births could be registered, on oath, and the earliest of the 46 recorded under this provision was 1821. Marriages were not centrally registered until 1884. certificates cost £5.25 including £2 search fee: from General Registry, Finch Road, Douglas. Opening times:- Mon.–Fri. 9a.m. to 1.00p.m. and 2.15p.m. to 4.30p.m.

Scotland

Registration did not become compulsory in Scotland until 1855, but Scottish Certificates have always been more detailed.

In addition to the information given on English Certificates, the following is stated:

(i)   Birth. date and place of parents' marriages (1855 and 1861 onwards).
      (1855 certificates also state parents' ages and birthplaces).
(ii) Marriage. Mothers' names.
(iii) Death. Both parents' names.

The Registers of Births, Marriages and Deaths are at New Register House, Edinburgh, where the original registers may be consulted on microfiche and not just the indexes as in England. The fee is £16.00 per day, although a limited number of places are available at £12 per day, if booked in advance, (also see below).

A microfilm copy of the indexes (1855–1920) is held at the Society of Genealogists.

Other Records Available for Consultation on Microfilm and Microfiche

(a)   Old Parish Registers (1553–1854), BUT incomplete.
(b)   Census (1841–891).
(c)   Marine Register of births and deaths (from 1855).
(d)   Service records of births, marriages and deaths (from 1881).
(e)   War Registers (from 1899): Deaths:
      1. Boer War (1899–1902).
      Warrant Officers, N.C.O.s and men (Army).
      2. World War I (1914–1919).
      Petty Officers and men (Royal Navy).
      3. World War II (1939–1945).
      Armed forces BUT incomplete.
(f)   Consular Returns: Certified copies of:
      1. Births and deaths (from 1914).
      2. Marriages (from 1917).
(g)   Births, Marriages and Deaths in foreign countries (1860–1965). Compiled on the basis of information supplied.
(h)   Adopted Children Register (from 1930). No entries for persons born before October 1909.
(i)   Air Register of births and deaths (from 1948). Events occurring on aircraft

registered in the U.K. where deceased or child's father usually resident in Scotland.

(j)   Divorces (from May 1984).

The statutory index of births, marriages and deaths (1855 to date) and the old Parish Register indexes of births and marriages (1553–1854) are available on computer and having located the desired index reference, the microfilm/microfiche can be self-accessed.

Daily, 4 weekly, quarterly and annual 'searches' may be purchased.

Certificates cost £10 for personal application and £12 by post, if the search is successful. Otherwise a charge of £3 is made [£5 for postal enquiries] and the balance refunded.

Opening hours are:- Mon. – Thurs. 9.00a.m. – 4-30p.m.: Fri. 9.00a.m. – 4.00p.m.

IRELAND

Registration did not generally begin in Ireland until 1 January 1864. Non Roman Catholic marriages were, however, registered from 1 April 1845 and one earlier Marriage Register exists, the German Protestant Church, Dublin (1806–1837).

Registers of births, marriages and deaths before 31 December 1921 for the whole country are held at the General Register Office (Oifig an ArdChlraitheora), Joyce House, 8–11 Lombard Street, Dublin 2. Opening Hours, Mon. – Fri. 9.30a.m. to 12.30p.m. and 2.15p.m. to 4.30p.m.

After 31 December 1921, the records for Northern Ireland are separate (see below). The cost of a Particular Search for any period not exceeding 5 years is IR £1.50 but the information supplied must be sufficient to enable an entry to be positively identified: in the case of a birth the names of both parents, including the mother's maiden name, are required.

The cost of a certificate (including particular search fee) is IR £5.50. A General Search may be made PERSONALLY, on payment of the following fees:

Births or Deaths: any number of successive hours not exceeding 6: IR £12.00.

Marriages: any number of successive days not exceeding 6: IR £12.00.

Other Registers and Records (N.B. To 31//12/1921 All Ireland: thereafter excluding Northern Ireland).

Births and Deaths at Sea (from 1/1/1864).

Consular Returns, Births and Deaths abroad (from 1/1/1864).

Births, deaths and Marriages (Army Act 1879).

Original Certificates of Marriages by Special Licence (Act of 1871).

Original Certificates of Roman Catholic Marriages (1/1/1864–30/9/1881)

Adopted Children (from 10/7/1953).

Certain marriages at Lourdes (Act of 1972).

Northern Ireland

(i.e. Antrim, Armargh, Down, Fermanagh, Londonderry and Tyrone).

Registration of Births and Deaths since 1864 and marriages since 1922 are held at The General Register Office, Oxford House, 49/55 Chichester Street, Belfast, open Monday—Friday 9.30 a.m.—4.00 p.m.
Other Registers available from 1922:-
  (a) Births and deaths at sea.
  (b) Consular returns of birthsand deaths. (N.B. Marriages from 1923.)
Service Department Registers date from 1927 and there is also a record of War Deaths for the period 1939 to 1948.
The Adopted Children's Register dates from 1931.
Records of marriages prior to 1922 are held by local Registrars (see also above).
A Particular Search for a specific entry, for a period of up to 5 years costs £2.00: certificates cost £5.50 A PERSONAL General Search costs £5.00 for any period up to 6 successive hours: however, it is necessary to book 6 months in advance.
(N.B. Overseas researchers should note that neither Office holds Emigration Records).

6. Census Returns

A census has been taken every 10 years since 1801, (except 1941), but it was not until 1841 that the returns had to be preserved. Consequently, for the previous four censuses, only the official statistics generally survive. Occasionally, however, the actual returns did survive, and whilst it is true to say that, generally speaking the first census of practical use to the genealogist is 1841, you should check to see if you are one of those fortunate researchers whose ancestors lived in an area for which earlier returns have been found. The 1801 census for Winnick with Hulme (of which a brief extract is shown in Figure 11) includes a woman aged 92, who was therefore born 1708/9.

Figure 11. Extract from example of rare survival of 1801 census Winnick with Hulme, one of the ten townships of the Parish of Winwick, originally Lancashire, now Cheshire.

Ralph UNSWORTH Sen.	74	Farmer
Nancey UNSWORTH	38	
Ralph UNSWORTH	11	
Peter UNSWORTH	9	
John UNSWORTH	7	
Robt UNSWORTH	4	
Marshall BROWN	19	Servant
Margret GORST	18	Servant

In England and Wales, public records are generally available after 30 years but certain records which contain sensitive personal information, including censuses, are subject to extended closure and do not become available for 100 years. The latest census which can currently be consulted in person is therefore 1891.

However, the General Register Office will extract the ages and places of birth of named persons at a specific address in the 1901 census for England and Wales, provided that written permission of the person(s), or a direct descendant, is produced and a declaration must be signed that the information will not be used in litigation. An application form (CAS 1/C) can be obtained from St. Catherine's House. This procedure is expensive and therefore advisable only if there is no alternative source. (Current cost − September 1994 − £16.75 + VAT £2.93. [N.B. Applications from abroad − including the Channel Islands and the Isle of Man − are not liable to VAT.] Unfortunately, almost all Irish censuses up to and including 1891, were destroyed in 1922, but the censuses for 1901 and 1911 may be consulted. Here too, there are exceptions, a few returns survived for 1841 and 1851.

It is easier to describe the later censuses first, 1851 (taken on the night of 30 March), 1861 (7 April), 1871 (2 April), 1881 (3 April, 1891 (5 April) all of which give the following information:

(a) Name of Place, Parish, and whether hamlet, village, town or borough.

(b) Number or name of house and its street or road; some enumerators did not enter the house number but (particularly in rural areas) simply the schedule number, with which it should not be confused.

(c) Names of persons present on Census night (dates as above).

(d) Relationship of each person to the Head of the Household.

(e) Matrimonial status.

(f) Age and sex.

(g) Rank, profession or occupation.

(h) Birthplace, (England and Wales by place and county, but generally country only (e.g. Scotland) for those born elsewhere.

(j) Whether blind, deaf or dumb (1871 included whether imbecile, idiot or lunatic).

The 1841 (7 June) census was unfortunately not so informative in several respects; using the letters above:

(b) Very few streets were numbered.

(d) Relationship to the Head of the Household not stated.

(e) Not given.

(f) Ages for those above 15 rounded down to nearest 5 years (e.g. recorded age 45; actual age could be 45, 46, 47, 48 or 49). Ages for those over 60 were often rounded down to the nearest 10 years.

(h) Birthplace simply indicated by "Yes" if born in the same county "No" if elsewhere in England and Wales. Those born in Scotland, Ireland etc. listed as such.

The differences between 1841 and 1851 (and later censuses) can be seen from the illustrations in Figures 12 and 13, respectively.

The marks made by enumerators should be noted:

/ at the end of each household.

// at the end of each building.

The exception is the 1851 census in which a line was drawn across the first 4 columns after the end of the building and a shorter line after the household.

Microfilmed (and for 1891 only microfiched) copies of the censuses are available for inspection at the Public Record Office, Chancery Lane, London WC2A 1LR, between 9.30a.m. and 5.00p.m. weekdays (including Saturdays).

Complete holdings of the various censuses for the county will usually be found in the County Record Office or the main county library and many reference libraries have copies for their local area, also on microfilm. Microfilm readers are easy to operate and you will be shown how to use one.

It is necessary to know an address to research a town with reasonable hope of quick success, although if the district in the town is known and this coincides with the sub-districts, you will find these listed on the title page of each index

Figure 12 EXTRACT FROM THE 1841 CENSUS (HO. 107/1092)
RUDGWICK, SUSSEX

PLACE	HOUSES		NAMES of each Person who abode therein the preceding Night.	AGE and SEX		PROFESSION, TRADE, EMPLOYMENT, or of INDEPENDENT MEANS	Where Born	
	Uninhabited or Building	Inhabited		Males	Females		Whether Born in same County	Whether Born in Scotland, Ireland, or Foreign Parts
Vicarage		1	Geo. Hathans	40		Clea		
			Willm. d-	35		Ind		
			Rebecca d		45	d		
			Sarah d		45			
			Catherine d		20			
			Jas. Medaway	40		Engraver		
			Martha d		15	Ind		
			Jesse Denk		14	J S		
Alabaster		1	Danl. Burger	55		Ag Lab		
			Elizabeth d		50			
			Hiram Denage	11		F S		
Common		1	George Earl	30		Bricklayer		
			Mary d		25			
			Peter d	4				
			Mary d		2			
			Mary Sayer		13	F S		
do		1	Noah Pellins	30		Ag Lab		
			Ann d		25			
			Willm. d	6				
			Henry d	5				
			John d	3				
			Harriett d		1			
			Willie d		?			
French?			Thos. Andrew	60		Ag Lab		
		1	Thos. Parker	55		-		
TOTAL in Page 13	5			12	13			

City or Borough of _____   *Enumeration Schedule.*

Parish or Township of *Rudgwick*

PLACE	HOUSES		NAMES of each Person who abode therein the preceding Night.	AGE and SEX		PROFESSION, TRADE, EMPLOYMENT, or of INDEPENDENT MEANS.	Where Born	
	Uninhabited or Building	Inhabited		Males	Females		Whether Born in same County	Whether Born in Scotland, Ireland, or Foreign Parts
Greenhurst		1	*Sarah Parker*	50			✓	
			...	10				
			John ...	14			✓	
...		1	*...*	50		✗	✓	
			Mary ...		50		✓	
			Mary Wharton		7		✓	
...		1	*...*	20		*...*	✓	
			Edmund ...	12				
			Mary ...		15			
...		1	*...Woods*	20		*...*		
			...	5				
			Mary ...		25			
			George ...	7				
			...	5				
			...		3			
			Will... ...	1				
			Sarah Waller		40	*Nurse*		
			Will... ...	9				
...		1	*...Shepherd*	25		*...*		
			Susan ...		20			
			Mary ...		80	*...*		
...		1	*...Thomas*	40		*...*		
			Hannah ...		40			
			Sarah do		9			
			George do	7				
TOTAL in Page 14		5		13	12			

Figure 13 EXTRACT FROM THE 1851 CENSUS (HO. 107/1648) HORSHAM, SUSSEX

	Parish or ~~Township~~ of		Ecclesiastical District of		City
	Horsham				Borough
H.U.S.B.	Name of Street, Place, or Road, and Name or No. of House	Name and Surname of each Person who abode in the house, on the Night of the 30th March, 1851	Relation to Head of Family	Condition	
67	South Street	Matilda Cockburn	Warder		
		James Dobson	Lodger	U	
		William Barker	Lodger	Mar	
68	East Street	Frances Sargant	Head	W	
69	South Street	Joseph Roberts	Head	Mar	
		Elizabeth D°	Wife	Mar	
		John D°	Son	U	
		Elizabeth D°	Daur	U	
70		Michael Keeling	Head	Mar	
		Ann D°	Wife	Mar	
		Sidney D°	Son		
		Hannah D°	Daur		
		Ann D°	Daur		
		John Sharp	Lodger	Wid	
		John Taylor	Lodger	U	
		Felix Morgan	Lodger	U	
		Stephen Fagan	Lodger	U	
		Barnard Fagan	Lodger	U	
		Andrew Wood	Lodger	U	
	4	John Morgan	Lodger	U	
Total of Houses I 3 U B				Total of Persons	

Borough of Horsham	Town of Horsham	Village of		
Age of		**Rank, Profession or Occupation**	**Where Born**	**Whether Blind, or Deaf and Dumb**
Males	Females			
	11		Surrey, Richmond	
62		Annuitant	Middlesex, Twickenham	
38		Cordwainer	Sussex, Worthing	
	63	Pauper, Charwoman	D° Framfield	
62		Furniture Dealer (Master)	D° Horsham	
	50		D° Billington	
26		Furniture Dealer (Journeyman)	D° Horsham	
	24	Glove Maker	D° D°	
33		Beer House Keeper	D° Rudgwick	
	32		D° Horsham	
4			D° D°	
	2		D° D°	
	6 mo		D° D°	
41		Butcher	D° Nuthurst	
41		Ag. Lab	D° Horsham	
45		Hawker	Ireland	
35		D°	D°	
30		D°	D°	
45		D°	D°	
35		D°	D°	
13	7			

and the amount of searching can be confined. There are street indexes for the larger towns. Enumeration districts vary in size: e.g. Preston (Lancs) 1851: Largest 325 houses with 2,164 inhabitants, smallest 114 with 616.

In rural areas it is possible to research whole villages and the surrounding countryside relatively quickly. Many Societies have started to index the 1851 census for their area and publish the results; over 500 indexes are known to exist.

The biggest and most ambitious project of all however, commenced in 1988, to index the whole of the 1881 census for England and Wales. Scotland was included later. The Genealogical Society of Utah (with permission of HMSO) lent microfilm or photocopies to volunteer transcribers, most of the labour being provided by members of family history societies. The results are transferred to a computer data base. The position at 30 January 1995 is that 97% of England and 87% of Scotland have been transcribed, of which 80% and 48%, respectively have been data entered. Wales, the Channel Islands and the Isle of Man are 100% complete. The colossal achievement of this project can be guaged from the number of entries,which will exceed 30,000,000! The data is on microfiche, initially arranged by county and then by surname and given name. Ultimately, when all counties have been completed, a national index will be produced. The appendix shows those counties for which microfiche indexes, which may not be purchased by individuals, are available at 30 September 1994. The census room at the P.R.O. receives copies, for England and Wales, as published.

All details on censuses should be noted including visitors and servants. Families frequently obtained the latter from where their parents lived and a servant's birthplace can, therefore, sometimes provide a clue.

If you cannot find the address bear in mind that the street, name or house numbers may have been changed between the date of the record you have and the date of the census. A local directory (see Chapter 11) may help to solve the problem.

The experienced family historian will not confine himself to one surname but will make a comprehensive search looking for the surnames of married daughters and wives' maiden names. He will also note down the neighbours, not only to provide background information about the environment, but to detect married children living nearby.

The problem of illiteracy runs like a thread through all records and the census is no exception, spelling variants will again be found and ages cannot be relied upon. Some ladies appear to have found the secret of retaining their youth and age less than 10 years between censuses.

Often overlooked, but valuable in finding out for example whether a nonconformist chapel existed prior to 1851, is the Ecclesiastical Census for that year. Although purely voluntary most places of worship made returns which show name, denomination, place, date of its consecration or erection, space available for worship, the minister or other official, the estimated attendances on 30 March 1851 and the average attendances in the previous year (some figures appear wildly optimistic).

Scottish records are at New Register House, Edinburgh (see page 33). The censuses for 1901 and 1911, and the survivals of previous returns, for the whole of Ireland are at the National Archives of Ireland, Four Courts, Dublin 7. Returns for the Channel Islands are available in London and additionally, for Jersey at the Societé Jersiase, The Museum, Pier Rd, St Helier and for Guernsey at Royal Court House, St. Peter Port.

The Family History Centres of the Latter-day Saints Church provided a service whereby any of the census reels available for the British Isles may be ordered at a cost of £2.55 per reel, which entitles you to free use of that reel at the library for four weeks.

Bibliography

Census Returns 1841–1881 on Microfilm: A Directory to Local Holdings, J.S.W. Gibson, FFHS.

Marriage, Census and Other Indexes for Family Historians, J.S.W. Gibson, FFHS.

An Introduction to ...The Census Returns of England and Wales, Susan Lumas.FFHS.

Making Use of the Census, Susan Lumas. P.R.O. Readers' Guide No.1.

Pre-1841 Censuses and Population Listings, C.R.Chapman.

Index to Census Registration Districts, M.E.Bryant Rosier, FFHS.

Census Records for Scottish Families, Gordon Johnson, Association of Scottish Family History Societies.

APPENDIX

Indexes Published on Microfiche at 30 January 1995. [May not be purchased by individuals.]

ENGLAND: Bedfordshire, Berkshire, Buckinghamshire, Cambridgeshire, Cornwall, Devonshire, Dorsetshire, Gloucestershire, Herefordshire, Hertfordshire, Huntingdonshire, Leicestershire, Northamptonshire, Oxfordshire, Royal Navy, Rutland, Shropshire, Somersetshire, Suffolk, Warwickshire, Westmorland, Wiltshire and Worcestershire.

SCOTLAND: Aberdeenshire, Banffshire, Berwickshire, Bute, Clackmannanshire, Dumfries-shire, Kincardineshire, Kinross-shire, Kirkcudbright, Moray/Elgin, Nairnshire, Orkney, Peebles, Roxburgh, Selkirk and Wigtownshire.

WALES: Every County.

CHANNEL ISLANDS and ISLE OF MAN: All.

7. Parish Registers, Bishops' Transcripts and Marriage Licences

Significant Dates

The earliest Registers date from 5 September 1538 when Thomas Cromwell, Vicar General to Henry VIII, ordered that every wedding, christening and burial in the Parish should be recorded. The entries were generally on paper and sixty years later in 1598 these Registers were ordered to be copied onto parchment, but the wording of the Act was unfortunate. It was ordered that entries from the old Registers should be copied "but especially since the first year of Her Majesty's reign". This gave the lazy an excuse to copy only from 1558 and that is why many Registers begin with that year. The 1598 Act approved a provincial constitution of Canterbury of 1597, which provided that, within a month after Easter, transcripts of the Registers for the previous year should be sent to the bishop. The earliest Bishops' Transcripts, therefore, normally date from 1597. When Civil Registration commenced in 1837, many incumbents ceased to send copies, but some conscientious clergy continued to do so for some years afterwards. The importance of Bishops' Transcripts is that they provide a second record, which may have survived when the Parish Register has perished. Even if the Register exists the corresponding B.T. entry should be checked because it sometimes includes additional information.

An unfortunate gap occurs in many Parish Registers during the Commonwealth period 1648–1660. Registers were often not properly maintained and the quality and completeness of the record (if any) varies considerably with the area.

The inexperienced searcher will find some dates in Registers baffling and a short digression is appropriate to consider the dating system, which is a fascinating study in itself.

Charles II left his exile in France on 5 June 1660 and landed at Dover on 25 May. Although having many claims to fame, time travel was not one of them and he could only achieve, what at first appears, a remarkable feat with the aid of the different calendars in use on the Continent and in England.

In England the (Old Style) Julian calendar was still in use whereas most of the Continent had adopted the (New Style) Gregorian calendar in 1582, as had

Scotland in 1660. Moreover, the Old Style calendar started the year on 25 March instead of 1 January. England had realised that it was "out of step" which is why some Registers have dates recorded e.g. 22 February 1722/3 (i.e. 1722 Old Style, 1723 New Style).

The Julian calendar was, by 1751, incorrect by 11 days and Chesterfield's Act, passed in that year, therefore, decreed not only that the following 1 January should be the first day of 1752 but that 2 September should be followed the next day by 14 September. The effect for successive years, therefore was:

1750 commenced 25 March 1750—ended 24 March 1750/1

1751 commenced 25 March 1751—ended 31 December 1751

1752 commenced 1 January 1752—ended 31 December 1752

(11 September days missing)

Bankers, however, have refused to have their year truncated and the financial year due to finish on 25 March was extended by 11 days to 5 April. This anomalous Financial Year continues to this day since no Chancellor since has had the nerve to cut short one of his years.

The next significant date is 25 March 1754, when Hardwicke's Act passed the previous year, came into force. Its stated objective was "An Act for the better prevention of clandestine marriages" and in this it was largely successful. Henceforth, all marriages had to be performed in the Parish Church or designated Parochial Chapelry except those involving Quakers and Jews, who were already keeping satisfactory records. It may surprise you to learn that prior to 1929 marriages could be contracted by boys from the age of 14 and girls from the age of 12. There had for many years been two ways to notify intention to marry, either by Licence or by the publication of Banns. Many clergymen were, however, lax and often married persons from distant parishes, who had not resided in their parishes for the requisite period and apparently without the calling of banns.

The Hardwicke Act ordered that all marriages must be preceded by the calling of Banns or by Licence, that parental consent was required by minors and that registers of banns must be kept. The importance of the banns register should be realised. Occasionally information is given which is not in the marriage register and where the bride and grrom were of different parishes the banns were read in both so that there is a record of intended marriages in other parishes, which would otherwise be difficult to find. Note, that banns denote an intention to marry, this does not mean that the marriage necessarily took place, though most did, and it is still necessary to trace the marriage entry.

In 1783 a Stamp Duty of three pence was imposed on every entry recorded in the parish register. Taxation is inevitably followed by evasion, paupers were exempted from the tax and the number of paupers recorded in the registers rose dramatically. Undoubtedly some people avoided the tax by not having their children baptised. Clearly the measure was unsuccessful as a revenue producer and the Act was repealed in 1794.

Rose's Act of 1812 provided for separate registers to be kept for marriages and burials respectively on specially printed forms.

Information

Prior to 1754 many registers are a hotch potch. Pages of baptisms may be interspersed with marriages and burials, sometimes pages include all three. The years covered for each record in the register may be different.

Baptisms

Until 1812 entries were on blank leaves. The information given varies from the simple entry of the name of the child, generally (but not always) followed by the name of the father. Some Registers give the name of the mother in addition. The most helpful include the father's occupation and some include places where the parents lived outside the parish and occasionally the date of birth is stated. More rarely details of grand-parents are given. it is a pity that so few scribes were this conscientious.

After 1812, the printed forms provide 8 baptisms per page with columns for: child's christian name, christian names of parents, father's surname, father's occupation and address, and by whom baptised.

Marriages

Until 1753 also on blank pages. From 1754 in a separate printed Register with spaces for: the names of the parties, their status (bachelor, spinster, etc.), their parishes, and the groom's occupation. The entries were signed by both parties, two or more witnesses and the officiating minister. Those who were illiterate made their marks, although there is some evidence that a mark did not always indicate illiteracy. It is, of course, very useful to know whether or not an ancestor could sign his name and the names of the witnesses are most important and should always be noted. These were often relatives and may provide a vital clue to family relationships.

It should also be stated whether the marriage was by licence and if an ancestor of yours did obtain a licence to marry you may be fortunate and obtain further information.

The licence itself was presented to the parson and few survive, but the associated allegations, bonds and registers of licences kept in the issuing office are much more likely to be extant and many have been published. The allegation (required until 1823) was a sworn statement that Canon Law had been observed and that there was no legal impediment to the proposed marriage. Two bondsmen were required to lodge securities (from circa 1579) that parents or guardians had given their consent and that there was no present or pending impediment. One bondsman was usually the groom and the other often a relative. The information required varied with the diocese but frequently included, in addition to the groom's and bride's names, their status (i.e. bachelor, widower, spinster or widow), ages (particularly of minors), occupations, places of residence and the church where the marriage was to be celebrated. If therefore the Parish Register indicates marriage by licence a search should be made for the associated documentation first consulting any indexes available, which should also be searched whenever difficulty is experienced in tracing a marriage. It is a mistake to assume that only gentry obtained licences.

An example will illustrate the value better than description:

> 2 January 1829 Edmund Hills, Hartfield, labourer, 20 (with consent of Wm. Hills, Hartfield, publican) and Mary Anne Pelling, West Hoathly, spinster, 20 (with consent of Thomas Pelling, West Hoathly, labourer, her father).

J.S.W.Gibson's book (see Bibliography) shows, for each county, the licences available, where located and whether published.

Burials

Until 1813 usually only the name is given with the addition of the name of the father in the case of an infant burial. Absence of this additional data does not imply an adult burial.

Once again some registers are more informative, stating ages, and sometimes additional detail, such as widow of ....

After 1813 there are eight entries per page with spaces for: name, abode, date of burial, age and officiating minister.

In 1678 an Act passed to benefit the wool trade requiring that "no corpse of any person (except those who shall die of the plague) shall be buried in any shirt, shift, sheet or shroud...... other than what is made of sheep's wool only".

An affidavit had to be sworn to that effect and penalties were imposed for non-compliance. The Act was not repealed until 1814, but the practice had fallen into disuse long before that date.

Copies of Registers and Indexes

You can save yourself much time and trouble if, before you begin your search, you find out whether the Register has been printed or copied and if so for what period. If it has been then often it will have been indexed and you will be able to extract all entries for the name(s) you want, readily and quickly. Most published works have concentrated, for obvious reasons, on the earliest records for a particular Parish and a convenient stopping point for many was 1812, when as already described the form in which the Registers were kept was altered. There is, therefore, a period from 1812 to 1837 (when Civil Registration started) when research is less easy.

Marriages are usually the most difficult area of research since many took place in the bride's Parish, and her name will not be known. In the event of parental disapproval, or for some other reason the marriage may not have taken place in either spouses' Parish but elsewhere, theoretically after the required period of residential qualification.

One of the first genealogists to recognise the need for Marriage Indexes was Percival Boyd, who worked on an index for 30 years prior to his death in 1955, his aim being to include every marriage in Parish Registers from 1538 to 1837. His achievement, with aid from a dedicated band of helpers, in indexing perhaps 12%–15% of all marriages with coverage for some 4,200 parishes is remarkable. It is not surprising that the coverage of the index is variable from county to county ranging from almost 100% of Cornish Parishes to only 4% in Staffordshire, and it should be noted that even if a Parish is included in the index the extracts may only be partial. The index is housed in the library of the Society of Genealogists, which also holds the largest collection of copies of Parish Registers.

Recognising the value of Boyd's work, other equally dedicated genealogists have in recent times, started to compile indexes for counties or areas in which they are particularly interested. The recent Federation booklet (see Bibliography) lists more than 50 indexes in existence and still being compiled and there are a number of others planned. Fees vary from nothing to £5 minimum and the invariable rule is that applications must always be made by letter and be accompanied by a stamped addressed envelope. (N.B. It is unwise to assume the accuracy of indexed data-the actual record should be checked to be certain).

Where are the Registers and What is the Cost of Research?

Until recently a substantial number were still kept locally in the hands of the incumbent but the Parochial Registers and Records Measure 1978 has led to most of the older Registers now being deposited in the Diocesan Record Offices. The Office in which the records are deposited is usually also the County Record Office but not all Diocesan Registries are under the auspices of local authorities, e.g. The Borthwick Institute, University of York.

Before undertaking a journey to a distant Parish or Record Office there are a number of factors to consider, not least the potential cost. Incumbents still holding registers are legally obliged to permit access, at convenient times, but, from January 1995, are entitled to charge a searcher the following fees:

Baptisms, Burials and Marriages before 1837:
Up to one hour £11.00
Each subsequent hour or part thereof £9.00
Post-1837 Marriages .... No Charge
Furnishing copies of above (for every 72 words) £5.00

It should be emphasised that this scale of charges applies only to researches carried out personally. The incumbent is not obliged to:

(i) permit the register (or any other record) to be photocopied.

(ii) supply certificates on postal application.

(iii) make searches on behalf of an enquirer.

If he does research in response to a postal enquiry then he is entitled to charge for his time.

Therefore, whether making a personal search or requesting information by post it is prudent to ascertain how much you will be expected to pay. One way of dealing with the problem of a postal enquiry, and of advantage to both parties, is for the enquirer to state what he is seeking and to enclose a cheque for an amount in words "not exceeding X (whatever you are prepared to spend) pounds", leaving the numerical amount to be filled in by the incumbent.

Care of Archival Material

Parish Registers (and any other original documents which you may wish to consult) are irreplaceable and vulnerable, so always treat them with respect by observing the following rules. Whilst examining records:

(1) ALWAYS USE PENCIL. Never ink.

(ii) DO NOT eat, drink, smoke or chew.

(iii) DO NOT rest anything on the document, or run a finger or pencil down it. NEVER attempt to copy by tracing.

(iv) Turn pages carefully.

(v) Leave the document as you found it.

Remember you are an ambassador for those who come to research after you, the reception they receive may be coloured by what you have done, or failed to do. One bad impression will last longer than many good ones.

Local Record Offices

A brief introduction is all that can be attempted here. It is essential that all preparatory work be done prior to the visit and that adequate notes are taken with you, plus a folder and notepaper, which should be divided up into appropriate columns if you know in advance the type of record you will be consulting. Record Offices do not have the staff available to deal with detailed enquiries. Some have only limited space available for researchers so not assume that you can be accommodated. To avoid disappointment, telephone or write first to ascertain:

(i)   Whether the record you want is available.

(ii)   Whether it is necessary to book a place and if so whether one is available on the day of your proposed visit.

Many Record Offices publish lists of their holdings of Parish registers, Bishops Transcripts and other documents; these are invaluable if you anticipate doing a lot of research in a particular area. In many Offices you will not be permitted to take bags and briefcases into the search rooms. Most reference works (e.g. Discovering your Family History or Local Population Studies) have lists of all the Record Offices throughout the country. There is also a Federation booklet with sketch maps.

Scotland

The old parish registers in Scotland were often badly kept. The majority date from the eighteenth century. There are also a good number for the seventeenth century, but few for the sixteenth; the earliest is 1553. One bonus is that where a baptism is recorded the mother's maiden name is usually stated. Unfortunately there is a dearth of burial or death records. In Scotland there are no County Record Offices and the Registers deposited are at New Register House, Edinburgh (see page 34 for details of "global" fees covering all records).

ꞏ The Church of the Latter Day Saints has compiled a county index to the old parish registers of baptisms and marriages on nanofiche (compact microfiche). Miscellaneous Records ('blotter' and 'scroll' records) have also been indexed. The indexes are available at New Century House and Family History Centres. [See Appendix.]

Ireland

After the disestablishment of the Church of Ireland an Act of Parliament decreed that its registers were to be deposited at the Four Courts Dublin, which unfortunately was burned in the "troubles" of 1921/2. Only four registers survived the holocaust but some registers had not been deposited and copies had to be made of others. The Handbook (see Bibliography) lists more than 650 known extant registers by county, stating the earliest year for which baptismal registers are known to exist (the oldest being St. John's Dublin, 1619). A number have been published. There are similar lists for the Presbyterian Registers (200+, oldest 1674) and Roman Catholic (1,000+, oldest 1690).

Roman Catholic Registers, which mostly remain with the church, are generally of later date, particularly for rural parishes, some of which do not commence until the 1860's. Microfilm copies of pre-1880 registers are held at the National Library Dublin.

The parish graveyard was frequently a common resting place for all denominations and burial entries may well be found in the registers of the established church.

Channel Islands

Jersey

The original registers are still in the charge of the parish rectors. Most are in French; the earliest (St.Saviour) dates from 1540. All the registers are being indexed by the Channel Islands Family History Society and enquiries should be addressed to the Secretary. There is also a register for the garrison of Elizabeth Castle 1714 – 1817: an indexed photocopy is in the Library of the Societé Jersaise.

Guernsey

The Priaulx Library specialises in Family History and has a comprehensive collection of parish registers on microfilm. Opening Hours Mon. – Sat. 9.30 a.m. – 5p.m.

Isle of Man.

The majority of Anglican Registers commence in the seventeenth century. The original registers were called into the General Registry and copied. These copies are included on the IGI.

Bibliography

National Index of Parish Registers:

Vol. 1*		*General Sources of births, marriages and deaths, before 1837.* (Indexed in Vol. 3).
Vol. 4		*Kent, Surrey and Sussex.*
Vol. 5*		*The West Midlands: Gloucestershire, Herefordshire, Oxfordshire, Shropshire, Warwickshire and Worcestershire.*
Vol 6*	Part1	*Staffordshire.*
Vol. 7		*Cambridgeshire, Norfolk and Suffolk.*
Vol. 8	Part 1.	*Berkshire.*
	Part 2.	*Wiltshire.*
Vol. 9	Part 1.	*Bedfordshire and Huntingdonshire.*
	Part 2.	*Northamptonshire.*
Vol. 11*	Part 1.	*North East England Durham and Northumberland.*
Vol. 13		*Wales.*

An Introduction to...Church Registers, Lilian Gibbens, FFHS

Original Parish Registers in Record Offices and Libraries (Local Population Studies), 5 parts.

Bishops' Transcripts and Marriage Licences, Bonds and Affidavits, J.S.W.Gibson, FFHS

---

* Out of print at September 1994.

Marriage, Census and Other Indexes for Family Historians, J.S.W.Gibson, FFHS
Record Offices: How to Find Them, Jeremy Gibson and Pamela Peskett, FFHS.
The Phillimore Atlas and Index of Parish Registers, ed. C.Humphery-Smith.
Genealogical Research in Victorian London, West Surrey F.H.S.
Genealogical Research in Edwardian London – London Parishes.
Reading Old Title Deeds, Julian Cornwall, FFHS.
How to Read Local Archives, F.G.Emmison.

Scotland

In Search of Scottish Ancestry, G.Hamilton-Edwards.
Introducing .... Scottish Genealogical Research, D. Whyte.
Scottish Roots, Alwyn Jones.
National Index of Parish Registers:
   Vol. 12 *Sources for Scottish Genealogy and Family History,* D.J.Steel.

Ireland

Handbook on Irish Genealogy, Heraldic Artists Ltd

Jersey

Family History in Jersey, Marie-Louise Backhurst, Channel Islands Family
   History Society.

8. Other Parish Records

Space does not permit more than a brief reference to some of the additional records which may be found but what Tate describes as "the intimate connection between the parish and the poor" provides a rich source of information often unobtainable elsewhere and providing, perhaps more than any other source, an insight into the way of life of our forebears. Until the Poor Law Reform Act of 1834 the relief of the poor was the responsibility of the Parish and there were many Acts from 1388 onwards, of which the most important were:

(a) 1601 which ordered that the churchwardens and 2 to 4 other substantial householders be nominated yearly as overseers, who were authorised to deal with the relief of the poor, the funds being provided by taxation of the local inhabitants.

Overseers' Accounts may contain details of payment for rent, clothes, medical and funeral expenses etc., with the names of the recipients.

Churchwardens' Accounts include a wide variety of expenditure and may include payments to the poor and details of bastardy.

Poor Rate Books contain details of those who paid and can amount to a virtual census of the more prosperous parishioners.

John (Jose) Pelling (see figure 5) was not baptised at Rudgwick and his parents were unknown. he was, however, a farmer and thus liable to pay the Poor Rate. Working backwards through the Rate Book it clearly showed the farm passing successively from John to Mary, widow, and to Michael. It also showed that he took over his father-in-law's farm. Since the farms were named it was a simple matter to check their location on the Tithe map for the Parish, which clearly showed that the farms were adjacent, so Jose had married the girl next door. The map also indicated that there were Estate Papers, examination of which provided an unexpected bonus, detailed maps of each farm showing the name and location of each field, its name and acreage. This shows the value of researching the records of a Parish in depth; references were also found in both the Overseers' and Churchwardens' Accounts which shed much light upon the decline in the family's fortunes, as did entries in the Vestry Minutes which chronicle the administration of the Parish and may include, for example, Parish apprenticeships.

(b) 1662 which provided for settlement and removal. The Parish was responsible for those having a legal settlement there, which could be achieved in several ways, of which birth was one. This meant that until 1743/4 (after which a child acquired its mother's place of settlement) it was common practice for vagrant pregnant women to be hastened on from Parish to Parish so that the baby would become the responsibility of another.

Strangers could be removed by order of the Justices and anyone staying temporarily, for example for harvesting, had to have a certificate from his own Parish agreeing to take him back.

Successive Acts almost immobilised the poor so:

(c) The act of 1696/7 provided that poor persons may enter any Parish provided they possessed a settlement certificate, for which a Federation Vice President has coined the apt phrase "Pauper's Passports". The most iniquitous provision of this Act (not repealed until 1781/2) was that a pauper (and his wife and children) "shall wear upon the shoulder ...... a large Roman P together with the first letter of the name of the parish ....".

An ancestors misfortune can prove of great assistance to the family historian. The pauper was brought before a Magistrate and examined about his origins, parentage, and previous occupations.

These Examination and Removal Orders may survive at the Parish of removal or with the Quarter Sessions Records (usually to be found at the C.R.O.) which are themselves a rich source of genealogical information.

The 1834 Act brought Parishes together into Unions administered by guardians and their records often show payments to paupers to enable them to emigrate. The law relating to settlement was not substantially changed until 1876.

Bibliography

The Parish Chest, W.E.Tate.

Quarter Sessions Records for Family Historians: A Select List, J.S.W.Gibson, FFHS.

An Introduction to...Poor Law Documents Before 1834, Anne Cole, FFHS.

9. Non-Conformist Records
The Public Record Office

Many people know that their ancestors were non-conformist (which for the purposes of this chapter embraces all denominations other than the Church of England), and those who do not must always bear the possibility in mind, particularly when researches in relevant C. of E. records have proved unfruitful. Non-conformists do appear in C. of E. Records and the use of born (instead of baptised) and interred (instead of buried) may be an indication of non-conformity.

It cannot be denied that non-conformist research is more difficult. Minority faiths were often persecuted and even in more tolerant times restrictions were placed on their activities. The subject of non-conformity is vast and space is sufficient only to give some indication of the records available.

A commission was appointed in 1837 to consider the state and authenticity of non-parochial registers. It recommended that all records should be sent to the Registrar General and many were surrendered at that time. These have now been transferred to the Public Record Office and microfilmed. The Catholics refused initially, and so did the Society of Friends (Quakers).

One important Register of births surrendered was that kept by Dr. William's Library, which was commenced in 1742 by a combined body representing Presbyterians, Baptists and Congregationalists, after concern had been expressed at the failure of many congregations to keep proper records. The importance of Hardwicke's Act has already been stressed and between 1754 and 1836, all marriages, except for those of Quakers and Jews, had to be celebrated by the Church of England in order to be considered legally valid. Monumental Inscriptions are very important for non-conformists since they may in fact be the only record available. It was not until 1880 that non-conformists ministers were given the right to perform burials in C.of E. churchyards. The best known non-conformist burial ground is at Bunhill Fields, which was the main non-conformist burial ground for the London area for more than 200 years. An index is available in the Guildhall Library.

Roman Catholics

Only 79 Catholic Registers were deposited in 1837, (many more have been deposited since), of which Yorkshire accounted for 46, Durham 12 and

Northumberland 10. In Lancashire only 1 out of 71 was deposited, and there were none from 16 counties. Those not deposited remained with the Church.

An increasing number are being deposited in Record Offices and the Catholic Record Society has published much valuable material. It should be noted that the Record Society is not a genealogical society, but there is now a Catholic Family History Society, which is a member of the Federation.

Baptists

Baptist records are perhaps the least extensive, 431 chapels (Yorkshire again having the largest number) surrendered registers in 1837, of which there is a complete list in Geoffrey Breed's book (see Bibliography).

United Reformed Church

Formed in 1972 by a union between the Congregational Church of England and Wales and the Presbyterian Church of England. the Presbyterian Historical Society of England combined with the Congregational Historical Society to form the United Reformed Church Historical Society, 86 Tavistock Place, London, WC1H 9RT.

The library is open, by arrangement, usually Tuesdays, Thursdays and Fridays: 10.30a.m.–4p.m. It is rich in 17th century material and contains more than 6,000 books and 2,500 pamphlets. Prospective visitors are requested to write or phone so that arrangements may be made. Written enquiries are dealt with by volunteer researchers.

(i) Congregationalists (also called Independents)

No less than 1,278 chapels surrendered Registers in 1837, Yorkshire providing 138, more than twice the total for any other county except London's 77. Some 40 Independent congregations did not accept the 1972 union and they are served by the old Congregational Library, 14 Gordon Square, London WC1H 0AG.

(ii) Presbyterians and Unitarians

194 Presbyterian registers were deposited (and 6 Unitarian). Lancashire was the leading county with 29 (and 2), nearly double that of the next county Yorkshire 15 (and 3). A number of Registers have been published.

Quakers

The Quakers founded by George Fox in the mid-17th century, were the most record-conscious of all Non-Conformists. Marriages with non-Quakers were forbidden and there was a very strict ban on cousin relationships. These strictures led to exhaustive enquiries about marriages for which parental consent was always required (until 1883), irrespective of the age of the parties. Three meetings were required before the marriage was contracted and the standard marriage certificate used from 1677 sometimes had as many as 40 witnesses. Before finally handing over all their registers in 1857,, digests were made of the entries which date from the early 1600's and include approximately 260,000 births. These are kept at the Library of the Society of Friends, Friends House, Euston Road, London NW1 2BJ.

Indexes available include:
Marriages in the digest registers (for the greater number of quarterly meetings);
Journal of Friends Historical Society, Vols. 1–53 (1903–75);
Deaths recorded in the Annual Monitor (1813–1892);
Collection of the Sufferings (prior to 1689);
Dictionary of Quaker Biography.

The library is open (excluding Public Holidays), Monday to Friday, 10a.m.–5p.m. Charges at time of writing: Personal searches £2 per hour, Proxy £8 per hour.

Quakers, like certain other denominations, refused to acknowledge months named after heathen gods and used an alternative dating system.

e.g. 25 March 1737 was 25 1Mo 1737
and 31 Dec 1737 was 31 10Mo 1737, but from 1752 January became accepted as the first month.

Jews

The Jews were originally expelled from England in 1290. Two principal groups have migrated to Great Britain since the 17th century.

(i) Sephardic – from Spain, Portugal and Italy.
(ii) Ashkenazi – from Eastern Europe, Bohemia, Germany and Holland.

They have settled quite widely throughout Britain specially in the larger towns and cities, where synagogues were established, records of the congregations are available. Searchers are advised to approach their local synagogue. The Jewish Museum, Woburn House, Upper Woburn Place, London WC1H 0EP or the Jewish Historical Society, 33 Seymour Place, London, W1H 5AP.

Methodists

It was not the wish of John Wesley (1703–1791) to separate from the Church of England and during his lifetime Methodist Chapels were called "Preaching

Houses", the parish church being used for baptisms, marriages and burials. The earliest registers date from 1795 when baptisms commenced in some chapels and burial grounds were also established. Following Wesley's death a number of schisms occurred and Figure 14 shows diagrammatically the divergences and the eventual reunions.

Number of Registers surrendered (County with most)

Wesleyan Methodists	697	(Yorks. 138)
Primitive Methodists	97	(Yorks. 17)
Methodist New Connexion	48	(Yorks. 15)
Bible Christians	29	(Cornwall 11)

The problem often is to identify to which splinter group a particular chapel or ancestor belonged. When exploring Methodist records it should be remembered that a man who was, say in 1840, a strong member of the Methodist New Connexion, could have started life as a Wesleyan and been baptised and perhaps married at a completely different chapel. Marriages present a particularly difficult problem. Between 1837 and 1899 many chapels were licensed for marriage only with the presence of a Registrar, who kept the official records. The Chapel record was optional and not always kept.

Figure 14 DIVISIONS OF THE METHODIST CHURCH

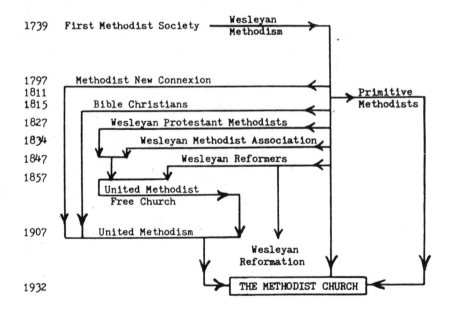

Public Record Office

The PRO has been mentioned in connection with many of the non-conformist records and it is appropriate to consider it briefly here. The PRO is split between 2 buildings (open 9.30 a.m.—5 p.m. Monday—Friday) and a reader's ticket is required:

(a) Chancery Lane (scheduled to close in 1996), containing legal records, PCC Wills (see next Chapter), non-conformist registers, and (from 1990) census returns.

(b) Ruskin Avenue, Kew (Richmond); containing mainly Departmental Records, e.g. Military, Naval and Merchant Shipping.

Bibliography

National Index of Parish Registers:
  Vol. 2 *Sources for Non-Conformist Genealogy and Family History,* D.J.Steel.
  Vol. 3 *Sources for Roman Catholic and Jewish Genealogy and Family History,* D.J.Steel.

Tracing Your Ancestors in the Public Record Office, Jane Cox and Timothy Padfield.

List of Non-parochial Registers and Records in the Custody of the Registrar General, Main Series (Births, Deaths and Marriages).

My Ancestors Were Quakers: How can I find more about them?, E.H.Milligan and M.J.Thomas.

My Ancestor Was Jewish: How can I find out more about him?, ed. Michael Gandy.

My Ancestors Were Baptists, Geoffrey R. Breed.

My Ancestors Were Congregationalists in England and Wales, D.J.H.Clifford.

10. Wills, Letters of Administration and Inventories

"Where there's a will there's a way", is often said in a different context, implying that if you have the determination you will succeed and genealogically speaking it is very apt.

Wills are the truest and most reliable genealogical record available and yet probably the least used. In some cases they are the only firm way of establishing family relationships where two persons of the same name lived in the same neighbourhood at the same time.

We are all familiar with the phrase "last Will and Testament" but a question seldom asked is what is the difference? The answer is simple, a Will was concerned with realty (real estate) and a Testament with personalty (personal property).

Just to confuse the issue, in Scotland the word Testament is always used but it must be appreciated that Scottish (Roman) Law is different from English. In Scotland a man can only alienate, that is freely dispose of, his estate if his wife and children do not survive him. Otherwise he can only dispose of part of it as follows:

WIFE (W) Living	CHILD/CHILDREN (C) Living	Share of Estate	Disposable
Yes	Yes	W. 1/3 C. 1/3	1/3
Yes	No	W. 1/2	1/2
No	Yes	C. 1/2	1/2

This system also originally applied in England but was gradually eroded until, by the end of the 16th century, the old rule applied only in the Province of York (until 1693), Wales (1696) and, strangely, the City of London (1726).

The Statute of Wills 1540 provided that Wills could be made by boys from the age of 14 and girls from the age of 12 (and these ages still apply in Scotland).

Anyone could make a Will except: children, lunatics, heretics, apostates, prisoners, slaves and married women. A married woman could not make a Will without her husband's consent until the Married Women's Property Act of 1882 and even that applied only to those married after 1 January 1883.

An English Will is revoked by a subsequent marriage, a Scottish Will is not but if a Scotsman omits to mention unborn children and a child is born after the Will is made, then it is revoked. A holograph Will, entirely in the deceased's handwriting, did not require witnesses (and is still recognised as valid in Scotland). Until 1838 Nuncupative (oral) Wills were valid if there were witnesses.

A Will names a person or persons, the executor(s) (a women is executrix), to carry out the deceased's (Testator or testatrix) wishes. The executor has to obtain an official document from the Court, the grant of probate, to prove he is the person legally authorised to administer the estate. If the deceased did not make a will then he is said to have died intestate and letters of Administration (usually abbreviated to "Admon".) must be obtained by the next of kin. Sometimes Letters of Administration are granted even when there is a Will because the executor has died or declined to act.

England and Wales

From 11 January 1858, the country was divided into civil probate districts and all Wills proved and Admons granted subsequently are held at the Principal Probate Registry, Somerset House, Strand, London WC2R 1LP. There the indexes may be searched free of charge. Wills may be viewed for 25p so that it is far cheaper to look at the details in a Will than to buy a death certificate. A photocopy of a Will may be obtained for the cost of photocopying.

For postal enquiries, form RK 1 may be obtained, from Somerset House: once completed the form should be sent to York Probate Sub-Registry, Duncombe Place, York, YO1 2EA: a 3 year search costs £2.

The annual indexes were printed, for use in the local probate registries. Prior to 1926 the jurisdiction of District registries covered a specific area; subsequently, executors may prove a will, or next of kin obtain letters of Administration, in any registry.

These sets of indexes (to 1928 or later) have now mostly been transferred to county record offices or major libraries, locations given in Probate Jurisdictions see Bibliography). They can too be used as a short cut to finding date of death for most men of any substance dying after 1857.

Prior to 1858 Wills in England had to be proved in the Ecclesiastical Courts (of which there were some 300) and it is the complex system of these which most people find confusing because of the difficulty of determining which Court had jurisdiction. The searcher will not normally know the reason why a Will was proved in a particular court and all courts should be searched. (In the order shown in the flow chart — Figure 15).

Figure 15 FINDING THE APPROPRIATE PROBATE COURT

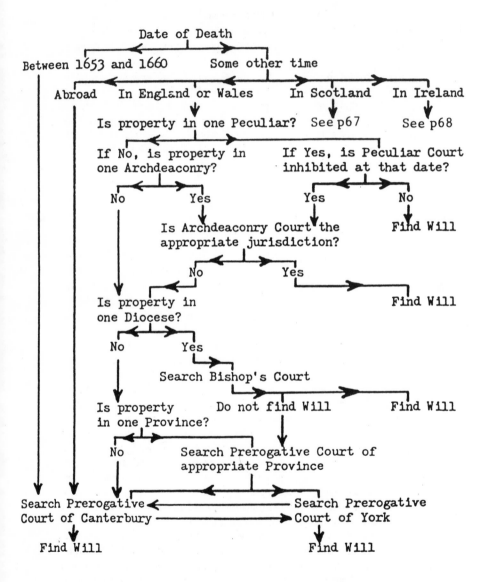

Organisation of the Church of England

The status of an Ecclesiastical Court is related to church administration which is as follows:

(a) The PARISH is the smallest unit having a vicar or rector.
(b) A RURAL DEANERY is an area consisting of a number (not usually more than 12) of parishes headed by a rural dean who is usually minister of one of its parishes.
(c) AN ARCHDEACONRY consists of a number of rural deaneries each in the charge of an archdeacon.
(d) A DIOCESE consists of several archdeaconries over which a bishop has authority.
(e) A PROVINCE is a large area of several Dioceses with the authority vested in an archbishop and until the Archbishopric of Wales was created in 1920 there were only two (Canterbury and York).

Probate Jurisdiction

The Courts of Jurisdiction can now be considered bearing the above hierarchy in mind.

(a) PECULIARS. The smallest probate divisions, which were, by ancient custom, exempt from the Archdeacon's and usually the Bishop's authority. A given Peculiar may consist of:

A single parish
Several Parishes, either adjacent or widely separated, which may be even in different counties.
A Manorial Court.
Universities and Colleges (e.g. Oxford and Cambridge).
Certain cities and towns.
At times Peculiar Courts were inhibited (i.e. closed) in which case the next superior Court exercised jurisdiction. Wills were normally proved in Peculiar Courts if the deceased's property was solely within that Peculiar.

(b) RURAL DEANS did not normally exercise probate jurisdiction but in some areas it was customary for them to do so under commission from either the Archdeacon (e.g. Richmond) or from the Bishop (e.g. Diocese of York).
(c) ARCHDEACON'S COURTS. If property was held solely within one Archdeaconry and if the Archdeaconry exercised its jurisdiction (the Bishop claimed jurisdiction over those which did not), then normally the Will was proved in the Court of the Archdeaconry.
(d) BISHOP'S DIOCESAN OR CONSISTORY COURTS. Granted probates where property was held in more than one archdeaconry but solely within the same diocese. in some dioceses the Bishop also claimed jurisdiction over the estates of noblemen and clergy within the diocese. A Commissary Court

was the name given to a Consistory Court which exercised the jurisdiction of an Archdeacon's Court.

(e) ARCHBISHOP'S COURTS. Granted probate where property was held in more than one diocese.There were two courts:

The Prerogative Court of Canterbury (PCC) which covered all counties not listed under PCY and South Lancashire prior to 1541 and the Prerogative Court of York (PCY) which covered Cheshire, Cumberland, Durham, Lancs., Northumberland, Notts., Westmorland and Yorks.

If property was held in more than one province then Canterbury claimed superior jurisdiction. In the period 1653–1660 all Wills were proved in the PCC.

The PCC also had jurisdiction over the estates of those who died overseas. Moreover, executors of people of standing often used a higher court than was necessary. The PCC is obviously by far the most important Court and indexes to its Wills 1383–1700 have been published. The Society of Genealogists has a card index relating to the period 1750–1800, covering approximately 500,000 Wills. This index is not open to public search but for a modest fee, staff of the Society will check for specific names on request.

The index has been published and may be purchased from the S.O.G..

PCC Wills are at the Public Record Office and PCY Wills are at The Borthwick Institute, York. Other Wills are to be found at the various County Record Offices. Probate Jurisdictions sets out in detail where the Wills for each county in England and Wales are to be found (see Bibliography). Before 1733 the note of probate at the end of a will is in Latin. You can usually pick out the names of testator and executor who proved the will and their relationship, the remainder being legal verbiage of no genealogical relevance.

Inventories

Prior to 1782, when probate or admons. had been granted, several persons were appointed to take a true and perfect inventory of the personal estate. Copies are normally available in the appropriate CRO; some are indexed. Each included all goods moveable and immoveable; clothes, wares, leases, farm stock, cut grass and timber, growing corn, cash rent and debts due. Excluded were lands, hereditaments and wife's paraphernalia (i.e. the clothes fitting to her degree) and in York also her bed and coffer. PCC inventories only survive between 1661 and about 1700.

In many counties the inventory was listed room by room, an example is illustrated and you will quickly realise that no other source is likely to give you such an insight into how your ancestors lived. You may think that you cannot read the example shown, but if you study it for a while you will see that it is: "A true and perfect Inventory, All and Singular the goods chattels and ? creddits of Richard Pelling, the Parish of Shipley in the County of Sussex husbandman" ...... and that the first item is ...... for his apparell and money in purse £2.00". It then

Figure 16 PART OF AN EIGHTEENTH CENTURY INVENTORY

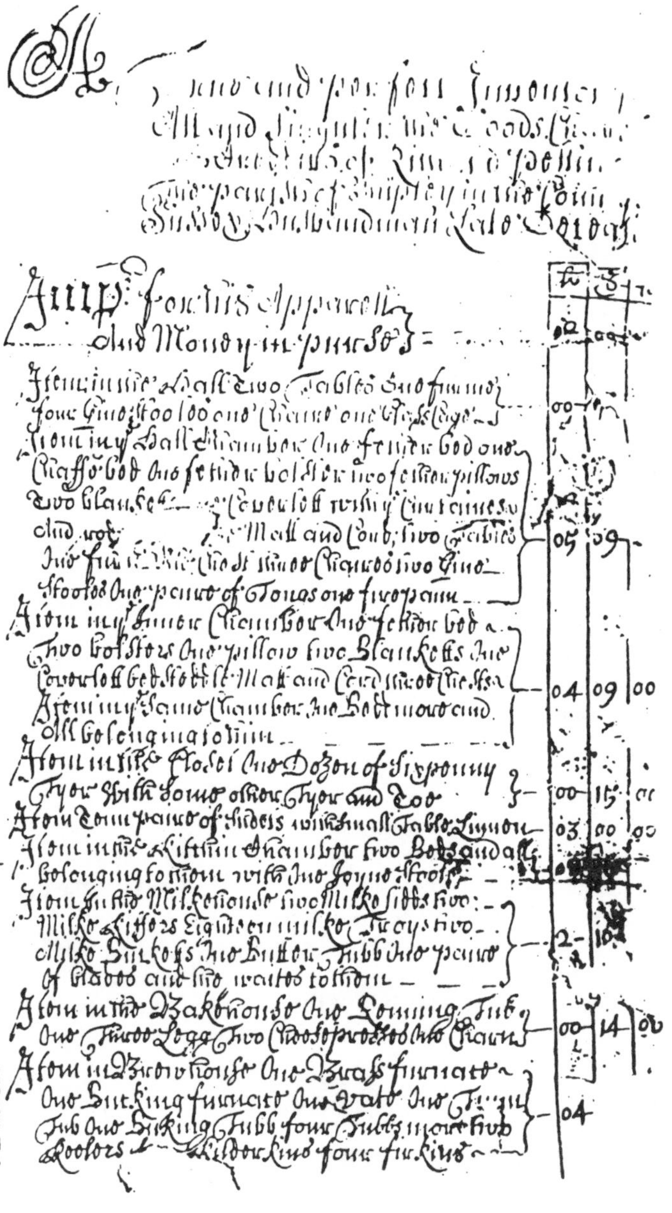

goes on to list the items in each room and given a start I am sure you will be able to decipher most of it.

Scotland

Until 1868 only moveable property could be bequeathed by will. After the Reformation the function of confirming testaments in Scotland (previously exercised by the bishop's courts) was assumed by Commissary Courts set up by royal authority (1566), that of Edinburgh having a local and a national jurisdiction, and the right to confirm the testaments of persons dying out of Scotland but having moveable estate in the country. The jurisdictions of the inferior commissary courts, originally 14 in number but later augmented, covered areas roughly co-terminous with the medieval dioceses. In 1823 the function of confirming testaments was invested in the Sheriff Courts, the commissary court of Edinburgh retaining a local jurisdiction until 1836.

The records of most Sheriff Courts, including their extant commissary records, pass the Scottish Record Office approximately ten to fifteen years after creation. The Office will advise you if records are still in the custody of the appropriate sheriff clerks.

Indexes are available in the Office's Search Rooms at the General Register House, Princes Street, Edinburgh, viz. Indexes to the Commissary Courts' registers of testaments, to 1800, published by Scottish Record Society and also available in may good reference libraries; Index to the personal estates of defuncts, 1827-67 (covering dates varying for different sheriffdoms), which indicate the existence of a confirmed testament in the appropriate Sheriff Court records; certain internal indexes to registers of inventories and confirmations post 1823, transmitted to the Record Office with Sheriff Court Records; the Calendar of Confirmations from 1876 to date.

Ireland

Irish Wills were also proved in diocesan courts, from 1536 to 1858, the Prerogative Court being that of the Archbishop of Armargh. Most Wills were destroyed in 1922 but indexes of 21,000 Wills and Admons. prior to 1800, which survived elsewhere, have been compiled. Copies of most of the indexes of those which were destroyed also survived. Post 1858 Wills have been proved at the Principal Probate Court and are held in the Principle Probate Registry in Dublin.

Wales

All locally proved Welsh Wills prior to 1858 are at the National Library of Wales, Aberystwyth.

Bibliography

A Simplified Guide to Probate Jurisdictions: Where to Look for Wills, J.S.W.Gibson FFHS (includes maps; covers whole of British Isles).

The Phillimore Atlas and Index of Parish Registers — also shows probate jurisdictions.

Latin for Local History, E.A.Goodber.

An Introduction to... Wills, Probate and Death Duty Records, Jane Cox, FFHS.

11. Other Useful Sources

Most of the sources described in the previous chapters will basically provide names, dates and addresses, although more may be gleaned from wills and parish records.

It is important to realise, however, that a recital of names, generation by generation, giving dates of birth, marriage and death, although no doubt interesting as a genealogy, is inadequate as a family history. Do not I urge you, simply become an ancestor collector. Try and build upon the "skeleton" of the basic information by placing the family events you have discovered into their broader historical context, which will involve investigation of the character and development of the area in which your ancestors lived.

A county history is a good starting point, but much more detail can be obtained from Directories, Newspapers and Magazines, of which libraries usually have a good collection for their locality.

Directories

Local Directories were published from 1780. Generally, a history and topographical description of the district is given and prominent persons and tradesmen are listed. The advertisements are particularly interesting, giving a true flavour of the period.

Newspapers

Having found the date of a birth, marriage or death, a check of the local paper may reveal more details; an obituary notice may contain a potted biography and the report of a funeral details of relatives. Even if the event is not recorded you will find out what were the items making the news which your ancestors may have read (if they could read, which you will probably have noted from other information), or which will have been the subject of gossip and may have influenced their lives or environment. The most comprehensive collection of National and other newspapers is held by the British Library. Provincial newspapers only included local news from the mid-18th century, and local newspapers only proliferated from the mid-19th century.

Of most use to the Family Historian, and by far the largest, is at Colindale Avenue, Colindale, London NW9 5HE. Open: Monday—Saturday, 10 a.m.—4.45 p.m. The collection consists of daily and weekly newspapers and periodicals: English provincial, Scottish and Irish from about 1700 and London from 1801. Commonwealth and foreign papers are also available. Prior to visiting, researchers are advised to phone to check whether the material sought is available. Normally, persons under 21 are not admitted. ·

School and University Records.

Often extensive biographical details are included, particularly in the printed University indexes. It is possible to trace several generations where sons of the family attended the same university, as often happened. Schools records may be found at the local Record Offices and the Society of Genealogists has an extensive collection for the Public Schools.

Apprentice Indentures

Youths were bound by indentures signed by a parent of guardian and the master to whom they were apprenticed, usually for 5 or 7 years. An example is shown in Figure 17. In 1710 a tax was imposed and central registration followed. The original records are in the P.R.O. Information given includes: Name of Apprentice and Master; father's name (or mother's if she was a widow) until 1760; and often residence.

The Society of Genealogists has an index covering the years 1710–1774.

Taxation

Our ancestors suffered, as we do, from the need of government to finance its activities. The earliest records are the subsidy rolls, which date from 1290 – of use to family historians between 1524 and 1640, when they provide periodic lists of the wealthier members of the community. Of greater use are the records of the Hearth Tax, which listed virtually all heads of households (with the number of fireplaces, or heated rooms, in their homes), taxing occupiers rather than owners. The tax was imposed in 1662 and lasted until 1689, but the records (mostly in the PRO, Chancery Lane), only survive between 1662 and 1674. It was succeeded by the Window Tax from 1696 to 1851, but this was only on the relatively well-off, and in any case very few records survive.

. The most useful tax lists for the 18th and 19th century are for the Land Tax. Although this was collected from the 1690s, most of the surviving records (in county record offices) are for the period 1780 to 1832, when payment of the tax was a voting qualification. For 1798 only, records for the whole of England and Wales (except Flintshire) are at the PRO (Kew). Names of owners of land and their tenants are given, annually, though occupants of cottages are often un-named.

Petitions

There are three other major sources for lists of names in the 17th century. Best

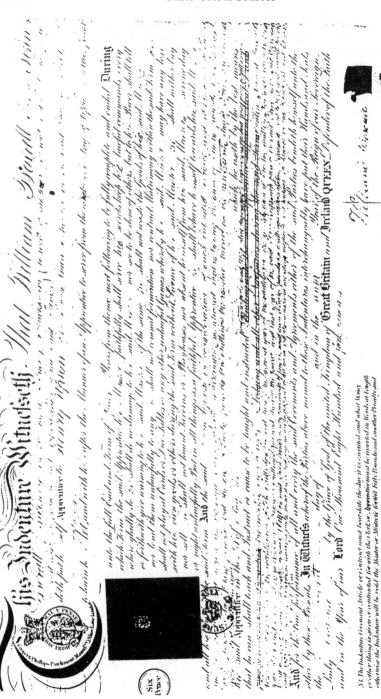

known are the Protestation Returns, of 1641, when most adult men signed a petition to the King in support of Parliament. A number of county lists have been published. The original lists are in the House of Lords Record Office. About the same time a collection was made in aid of Distressed Protestants in Ireland. This was widely supported, and lists of contributors are in the PRO (Chancery Lane). At the end of the century, a petition of support for William III (following assassination attempts) called the Association Oath Rolls was signed by all office-holders and a great many others; the lists are in the PRO (Chancery Lane).

Army and Naval Records

These are extensive and mainly in the PRO. As might be expected it is easier to trace an officer than other ranks.To trace a soldier successfully it is essential to know his regiment. Of particular interest for the Army is a list of retired officers compiled in 1828 which gives age when commissioned, date of marriage and births of children. The active list 1829–1919 includes, in addition, date and place of birth.

Bibliography

Guide to National and Provincial Directories of England and Wales before 1856, J.E.Norton.

Local Newspapers 1750–1920 – A Select List, J.S.W.Gibson, FFHS.

An Introduction to ...Using Newspapers and Periodicals, Colin R.Chapman, FFHS.

Alumni Cantabrigiensis, 10 Volumes, J. and J.A. Venn.

Alumni Oxoniensis, 8 Volumes, J.Foster.

Registers of the Universities and Schools of Great Britain and Ireland, P.M.Jacobs.

Land Tax Assessments c1690–c1950, J.S.W.Gibson and D.Mills, FFHS.

The Hearth Tax, Other Later Stuart Tax Lists and the Association Oath Rolls, J.S.W.Gibson, FFHS.

The History of Taxation, B.Sabine.

In Search of Army Ancestry, G.Hamilton-Edwards.

Records of Officers and Soldiers who have served in the British Army, PRO.

World War 1 Army Ancestry, N.Holding, FFHS.

The Location of British Army Records. A National Directory of World War I Sources, N.Holding.

Records of Naval Men, G. Fothergill.

My Ancestor was a Merchant Seaman. How can I find out more about him?, C.T. and M.J. Watts.

An Introduction to..Planning Research: Short Cuts in Family History, Michael Gandy, FFHS.

An Introduction to ...Occupations: A Preliminary List, FFHS.

Enquire Within, Pauline Saul, FFHS. (This is virtually an encyclopaedia for Family Historians.) N.B. The title of the hardback version — obtainable in book shops is *Tracing Your Ancestors: The A—Z Guide.*

12. Surnames

"What's in a name?......"; contrary to Shakespearian opinion, a great deal. You may have a common name, the derivation of which is fairly obvious, but as your searches progress names will appear on your tree, the origin of which may provoke your curiosity. The more unusual the name the easier research is and you can justifiably make a note of every occurrence of a rare one. Whatever the name it will stem from one of four basic roots:

1. Place.
2. Occupation or Office.
3. Personal (Relationship).
4. Nickname.

Place names are the most numerous, being derived from general places, Hill, Wood, Marsh or particular locations, London, Bedford, York. Originally place names were preceded by various prepositions, which in some cases have become attached: Attwell, Bywater, Underdown, Nash (atten ash). Provoked by an entry in the unreliable guide by Ewen — where my name was equated with that of Pilling, a place in Lancashire, which was clearly nonsense — I traced it to a small hamlet in Sussex, Peelings, which disappeared from the map in the second half of the eighteenth century. Even today, some 700 years after its first appearance there, the name is comparatively rare outside of Sussex, except in neighbouring Surrey.

In my researches I used The Place Names of Sussex, one of a series issued by the English Place-Name Society on a county basis, which cover the smallest of places, even farms, an example will show the value:

"Pellingbridge Farm is Pellyngesbregge 1425 Lewes Deeds, Pellyngbrege 1439 (Court Rolls), Pyllyngbregge 1441 (Court Rolls) and is to be associated with Simon de Pelling (1296 Subsidy Rolls), who perhaps came from Peelings in Westham ..."

The distribution of a particular place surname can be plotted from telephone directories, which may indicate the likely area or origin. Occupational names are sometimes obvious and a common ending is -er. Carter, Forester, Porter, and Turner, for example: less obvious, Chaucer, (French version of Hosier), Sainter (French saintier — bell founder), Scrimshaw (French scremmisseur — fencing master). The clothing industry accounts for some 165 names including, Dyer, Lister, Weaver and there are regional variations of the same process e.g. Fuller (S. & E.), Walker (W. & N.) and Tucker (S.W.)

Bardsley (see Bibliography), who was the pioneer in the field of surname origins, identified personal names derived not only from fathers (patronymics) but, to the consternation of the Victorians, to whom such names implied illegitimacy (by no means necessarily so), mothers (metronymics), Jackson, Dobson, Williams are obvious forms of the former, whilst the latter includes Annis (from Agnes), Catlin (Catherine), Ibbotson (Isabel) and Margetson (Margaret).

Nicknames fall into many categories: physical characteristics – Redhead, Fairfax, Ballard (bald), Armstrong; moral qualities – Doughty, Noble, Quant (knowledgeable); animals – Farr (bull), Buck, Lovett (wolf-cub); birds – Dove, Swallow, Ruddock (robin),; fish – Tench, Trout, Smelt (sardine); oaths etc. – Godber, Mordue, Pardoe.

In England there were no hereditary surnames before the Norman Conquest. They became inherited at any time in the subsequent 300 years, the north was less advanced than the south and in Lancashire and Yorkshire many surnames did not become hereditary much before 1400, and last of all was Wales.

In 1890 Guppy (see Bibliography), reasoning that farmers were the least mobile group counted their number in the Kelly's Directories and classified their names on a geographical basis thus:

1. General found in 30–40 Counties.
2. Common   „   „ 20–29
3. Regional „   „ 10–19
4. District „   „ 4–9
5. County   „   „ 2–3
6. Peculiar mostly confined to 1 County.

He found the most popular names to be:
1. Smith; 2. Brown; 3. Taylor; 4. Clark(e); 5. Robinson; 6. Johnson; 7. Wilson; 8. Hall; 9. Green; 10. Wright.

Scottish and Irish names have, as might be expected, their own peculiarities.

In some families, surnames of brides are adopted as christian names and where this happens it is invaluable to the researcher.

Bibliography

A Dictionary of English & Welsh Surnames, with special American Instances, C.W.Bardsley.

The Origin of English Surnames, P.H.Reaney.

A Dictionary of British Surnames, P.H.Reaney.

Discovering Surnames, J.W.Freeman.

The Homes of Family Names in Great Britain, H.B.Guppy.

13. Publicising Your Researches

Eventually you will have accumulated sufficient information to present a coherent account of your findings. Do not keep your discoveries to yourself. Someone, somewhere, may be waiting for a vital piece of evidence, which you have. The readily available excuse always is "but I haven't finished yet"; but, if you are an enthusiast you never will!.

The easiest way of informing other family historians about your findings is to write an article for the magazine of a Family History Society, editors of which are always looking for suitable material and they will be glad to give advice about presentation. In addition to the results your methods of research may be of interest to others faced with similar problems.

Family History News & Digest, the half yearly publication of the Federation of Family History Societies, contains a Digest section summarising most articles which have appeared in the Magazines of its members. This, coupled with the exchange journals between Societies, automatically ensures a wide coverage for your article and you could find yourself, as a result, exchanging information to your mutual benefit (as I have), with a reader in a distant part of the world.

If your forte is the spoken, rather than the written word, you might instead prefer to give an illustrated lecture to a Society located where your ancestors lived. If you do embark on this, thorough preparation is necessary, particularly with the production of visual material, which is essential for any talk lasting longer than 20 minutes.

Most effective, if you have the talent for it, is a tape/slide presentation, in which a slide sequence is accompanied by a commentary and/or additional sound material.

In due course the information accumulated may be far more than can be conveniently summarised within the confines of a single article and a larger publication should be considered. The costs of publication should be weighed against the likely sales; the former may be less than you think and the latter greater. Publications with strong local associations are likely to appeal to libraries. You would, however, be well advised to open a subscription list before committing yourself to much expenditure.

When you have at least three generations of family history recorded you may like to deposit a copy of your research papers in the document collection at the Society of Genealogists. This not only safeguards the information should you mislay your own papers but is a useful way of sharing research.

You may also discover other researches for the same name already in the collection. New additions are recorded in the Society's Journal.

Even if you do not feel able to pursue any of the options outlined above, try to share your researches with others by registering the names you are researching with the appropriate Family History Society and deposit copies of your pedigree charts, but, above all, meet others and share your enthusiasm together.

Family History has enriched my life leading me to new experiences of public speaking, teaching, writing and extensive travel: but for Family History I should never have found myself in a western saloon in the Colorado rocky mountains singing a cockney song to a bunch of cowboys ... but that is another story!.

You are warned that this pastime is addictive and may occupy your leisure hours for the rest of your life. May I wish you "good hunting" and who knows, we may find ourselves related.

I originally wrote those last words in 1979, since when for two readers it has proved prophetic.

14. Publications of Federation of Family History Societies (Publications) Ltd*

The Chapter Bibliographies include the works published by Federation of Family History Societies (Publications) Ltd, which are not generally available in bookshops. A comprehensive list of publications available at April 1995 is shown below; for price list please write (enclosing stamped, addressed envelope, or 3 International Reply Coupons) to FFHS (Publications) Ltd, 2-4 Killer Street, Ramsbottom, Bury, Lancashire BL0 9BZ.

Family History News and Digest (FFHS Publication)
Accommodation Register
Army Records for Family Historians
Beginning your Family History
Current Publications by Member Societies on Microfiche
Current Publications by Member Societies
Dating Old Photographs.
Family Historian's Enquire Within (Genealogical Encyclopaedia)
Forming a One-name Group.
GEDCOM Data Transfer (Moving Your Family Tree)
How to Tackle Your Family History (Leaflet)
Latin Glossary for Family Historians.
Some Medieval Records for Family Historians
Monumental Inscriptions
Practice Makes Perfect (A Genealogical Workbook).
Records of the R.A.F.
The Scots Overseas (Select Bibliography).
Was Your Grandfather a Railwayman?
Company and Business Records
Welsh Family History.
World War I Army Ancestry
More Sources of WWI Army Ancestry

---

* FFHS (Publications) Ltd is a wholly owned subsidiary of the Federation of Family History Societies.

AN INTRODUCTION TO ... SERIES

Census Returns of England and Wales.
Church Registers
Civil Registration
Occupations
Planning Research: Short Cuts in Family History.
Poor Law Before 1834.
Using Newspapers and Periodicals
Using Computers in Genealogy
Reading Old Title Deeds.
Wills, Probate and Death Duty Records

RAYMOND BIBLIOGRAPHIES & PERIODICALS

Genealogical Bibliography: Buckinghamshire.
Genealogical Bibliography: Cornwall
Genealogical Bibliography: Cumberland/Westmorland.
Genealogical Bibliography: Devon (2vols.)
Genealogical Bibliography: Dorset.
Genealogical Bibliography: Gloucestershire/Bristol.
Genealogical Bibliography: Hampshire
Genealogical Bibliography: London and Middlesex
Genealogical Bibliography: Lincolnshire
Genealogical Bibliography: Norfolk.
Genealogical Bibliography: Oxford.
Genealogical Bibliography: Somerset.
Genealogical Bibliography: Suffolk.
Genealogical Bibliography: Wiltshire.
British Genealogical Periodicals. Vol. 1, The Ancestor
British Genealogical Periodicals. Vol. 2, The Genealogist: Part 1, Sources. Part 2, Family Histories.
British Genealogical Periodicals. Vol. 3, Miscellanea Genealogica et Heraldica: Part 1, Sources, Part 2, Family Histories.
Occupational Sources for Family Historians.
English Genealogy.

GIBSON GUIDES FOR GENEALOGISTS

Poor Law Union Records:
  Volume 1.   South East & East Anglia.
  Volume 2.   The Midlands & Northern England.
  Volume 3.   South West England, The Marches & Wales.
  Volume 4.   Gazeteer of England & Wales.
Probate Jurisdictions
Bishops' Transcripts & Marriage Licences
Coroners' Records.
Hearth Tax Returns and Other Later Stuart Tax Lists.
Land & Window Tax Assessments.
Lists of Londoners.
Local Census Listings 1522–1930.
Local Newspapers: 1750–1920.
Marriage, Census and Other Indexes
Poll Books c.1695–1872
Quarter Sessions Records.
Record Offices: How to Find Them
Census Returns on Microfilm
Militia Lists and Musters (1757–1876)
Victuallers' Licences
Protestation Returns: 1641-2
Tudor and Stuart Muster Rolls.

APPENDIX. LDS FAMILY HISTORY CENTRES IN THE BRITISH ISLES

England

Avon

Bristol FHC, 721 Wells Road, Whitchurch, Bristol, Avon BS14 9HU (Tel. 0117-9838326).

Yate FHC, LDS Chapel, Wellington Road, Yate, Avon (Tel. 01454-323004).

Bedfordshire

St. Albans FHC, Corner of London Road/Cutenhoe Road, Luton, Bedfordshire LU1 3NQ (Tel. 01582-482234).

Berkshire

Reading FHC, 280 The Meadway, Tilehurst, Reading, Berkshire RG3 4PF (Tel. 01734-410211).

Cambridgeshire

Cambridge FHC, 670 Cherry Hinton Road, Cambridge CB1 4DR (Tel. 01223-247010).

Peterborough FHC, Cottesmore Close, Off Atherstone Avenue, Netherton Estate, Peterborough (Tel. 01733-263374).

Cheshire

Chester FHC, 30 Clifton Drive, Blacon, Chester, Cheshire CH1 5LT (Tel. 01244-390796).

Cleveland

Billingham FHC, The Linkway, Billingham, Cleveland TS23 3HG (Tel. 01642-563162).

Cornwall

Helston FHC, Clodgey Lane, Helston, Cornwall (Tel. 01326-564503).

Cumbria

Carlisle FHC, Langrigg Road, Morton Park, Carlisle, Cumbria CA2 5HT (Tel. 01228-26767).

Devon

Exeter FHC, Wonford Road, Exeter, Devon (Tel. 01392-50723).

Plymouth FHC, Hartley Chapel, Mannamead Road, Plymouth, Devon (Tel. 01752-668666).

Dorset

Poole FHC, 8 Mount Road, Parkstone, Poole, Dorset BH14 0QW (Tel. 01202-730646).

Essex

Romford FHC, 64 Butts Green Road, Hornchurch, Essex RM11 2JJ (Tel. 01708-620727).

Gloucestershire

Cheltenham FHC, Thirlestaine Road, Cheltenham, Gloucestershire (Tel. 01242-523433).

Forest of Dean FHC, Wynol's Hill, Queensway, Coleford, Gloucestershire (Tel. 01594-542480).

Hampshire

Portsmouth FHC, Kingston Crescent, Portsmouth, Hampshire (Tel. 01705-696243).

Hereford and Worcester

Redditch FHC, 321 Evesham Road, Crabbs Cross, Redditch, Worcestershire B97 5JA (Tel. 01527-550657).

Humberside

Grimsby FHC, Linwood Avenue, Waltham Road, Scartho, Grimsby, South Humberside DN33 2PA (Tel. 01472-828876).

Hull FHC, Hull Second Ward, 725 Holderness Road, Hull, North Humberside HU4 7RT (Tel. 01482-701439).

Isle of Man

Douglas FHC, Woodside, Woodbourne Road, Isle of Man (Tel. 01624-675834).

Isle of Wight

Newport FHC, Chestnut Close, Shide Road, Newport, Isle of Wight (Tel. 01983-529643).

Jersey (Channel Islands)

St. Helier FHC, Rue de la Vallee, St Mary, Jersey, Channel Islands (Tel. 01534-82171).

Kent

Maidstone FHC, 76b London Road, Maidstone, Kent ME16 0DR (Tel. 01622-757811).

Lancashire

Ashton FHC, Tweedale Street, Rochdale, Lancashire OL11 3TZ (Tel. 01706-526292).

Blackpool FHC, Warren Drive, Cleveleys, Blackpool, Lancashire FY5 3TG (Tel. 01253-858218).

Chorley FHC, 33-41 Water Street, Chorley, Lancashire (Tel. 01257-269332).

Lancaster FHC, Onangle Road, Morecambe, Lancashire (Tel. 01524-33571).

Rawtenstall FHC, Haslingden Road, Rawtenstall, Rossendale, Lancashire BB4 0QX (Tel. 01706-213460).

Leicestershire

Leicester FHC, Wakerleyad, Wakerley Road, Leicester LE5 4WD (Tel. 0116-2335544).

Lincolnshire

Lincoln FHC, LDS Chapel, Skellingthorpe Road, Lincoln LN6 0PB (Tel. 01522-680117).

London, Greater

Hyde Park FHC, 64–68 Exhibition Road, South Kensington, London SW7 2PA (Tel. 0171-589 8561).

Wandsworth FHC, 149 Nightingale Lane, Balham, London SW12 (Tel. 0181-673 6741).

Manchester, Greater

Manchester FHC, Altrincham Road, Wythenshawe, Manchester M22 4BJ (Tel. 0161-9029279).

Merseyside

Liverpool FHC, 4 Mill Bank, Liverpool, Merseyside L13 0BW (Tel. 0151-228 0433).

Midlands, West

Coventry FHC, Riverside Close, Whitley, Coventry (Tel. 01203-301420).

Harborne FHC, 38 Lordswood Road, Harborne, Birmingham B17 9QS (Tel. 0121-4279291).

Sutton Coldfield FHC, 185 Penns Lane, Sutton Coldfield, Birmingham B76 1JU (Tel. 0121-386 1690).

Wednesfield FHC, Linthouse Lane, Wednesfield, Wolverhampton (Tel. 01902-724097).

Norfolk

Kings Lynn FHC, Reffley Lane, Kings Lynn, Norfolk PE30 3EQ (Tel. 01553-67000).

Norwich FHC, 19 Greenways, Eaton, Norwich, Norfolk NR4 7AX (Tel. 01603-52440).

Northamptonshire

Northampton FHC, 137 Harlestone Road, Northampton, Northamptonshire (Tel. 01604-587630).

Nottinghamshire

Mansfield FHC, Southridge Drive, Mansfield, Nottinghamshire NG18 4RT (Tel. 01623-26729).

Nottingham FHC, Hempshill Lane, Bulwell, Nottingham NG6 8PA (Tel. 0115-9274194).

Shropshire

Telford FHC, LDS Chapel, 72 Glebe Street, Wellington, Shropshire.

Somerset

Yeovil FHC, LDS Chapel, Forest Hill, Yeovil, Somerset (Tel. 01935-26817).

Staffordshire

Lichfield FHC, Purcell Avenue, Lichfield, Staffordshire (Tel. 01543-14843).

Newcastle under Lyme FHC, PO Box 285, The Brampton, Newcastle under Lyme, Staffordshire ST5 0TV (Tel. 01782-620653).

Suffolk

Ipswich FHC, 42 Sidegate Lane West, Ipswich, Suffolk IP4 3DB (Tel. 01473-723182).

Lowestoft FHC, 165 Yarmouth Road, Lowestoft, Suffolk (Tel. 01502-573851).

Surrey/Middlesex

Staines FHC, 41 Kingston Road, Staines, Middlesex TW14 0ND (Tel. 01784-462627).

Sussex, East

Crawley FHC, Old Horsham Road, Crawley, East Sussex RH11 8PD (Tel. 01293-516151).

Sussex, West

Worthing FHC, LDS Chapel, Goring Street, Worthing, West Sussex.

Tyne and Wear

Sunderland FHC, Linden Road, Off Queen Alexandra Road, Sunderland SR2 9BT (Tel. 0191-528 5787).

Worcestershire (see Hereford and Worcester)

Yorkshire, North

Scarborough FHC, LDS Chapel, Stepney Drive/Whitby Road, Scarborough, North Yorkshire.

York FHC, West Bank, Acomb, York, North Yorkshire (Tel. 01904-785128).

Yorkshire, South

Sheffield FHC, Wheel Lane, Grenoside, Sheffield S30 3RL (Tel. 0114-2453231).

Yorkshire, West

Huddersfield FHC, Dewsbury Chapel, 86 Halifax Street, Dewsbury, Yorks (Tel. 01924-460929).

Leeds FHC, Vesper Road, Leeds, West Yorks LS5 3QT (Tel. 0113-2585297).

Wales

Clwyd

Rhyl FHC, Rhuddlan Road, Rhyl, Clwyd.

Appendix. *LDS Family History Centres*

Glamorgan, Mid-
Merthyr Tydfil FHC, Nanty Gwenith Street, George Town, Merthyr Tydfil, Mid-Glamorgan CF48 1NR (Tel. 01685-722455).

Glamorgan, South
Cardiff FHC, Heol y Deri, Rhiwbina, Cardiff, South Glamorgan CF4 6UH (Tel. 01222-620205).

Glamorgan, West
Swansea FHC, LDS Chapel, Cockett Road, Swansea, West Glamorgan.

Scotland
Dunfries and Galloway
Dumfries FHC, 36 Edinburgh Road, Albanybank, Dumfries.

Fife
Kirkcaldy FHC, Winifred Crescent, Forth Park, Kirkcaldy, Fife (Tel. 01592-640041).

Grampian
Aberdeen FHC, North Anderson Drive, Aberdeen, Grampian AB2 6DD (Tel. 01224-692206).

Highlands and Islands
Inverness FHC, 13 Ness Walk, Inverness, Highlands IV3 5SQ (Tel. 01463-231220).
Lerwick FHC, South Road, Lerwick, Shetland Islands (Tel. 01595-5732).

Lothian
Edinburgh FHC, 30a Colinton Road, Edinburgh EH4 3SN (Tel. 0131-337 3049).

Strathclyde
Glasgow FHC, 35 Julian Avenue, Glasgow, Strathclyde, G12 0RB (Tel. 0141-357 1024).
Kilmarnock FHC, Whatriggs Road, Kilmarnock, Ayrshire KA1 3QY (Tel. 01563-26560).
Paisley FHC, Campbell Street, Paisley, Johnstone, Strathclyde PA5 8LD (Tel. 01505-20886).

Tayside
Dundee FHC, Bingham Terrace, Dundee, Tayside DD4 7HH (Tel. 01382-451247).

Northern Ireland
Antrim/Down
Belfast FHC, 401 Holywood Road, Belfast, Northern Ireland BT4 2GU (Tel. 01232-768250).

Londonderry

Londonderry FHC, Racecourse Road, Belmont Estate, Londonderry, Northern Ireland.

Republic of Ireland

Dublin

Dublin FHC, Ireland Dublin Mission, The Willows, Finglas, Dublin 11, Republic of Eire (Tel. 00-353-4625609).

INDEX

Index

Index